Introduction

There is power in these pages. It is the power to create, with our children, a future where kindness, fairness, and consideration of others are the norm. It is the power to bond children and adults, children and schools, children and their wider communities. It is the power of a society to become what it can and should be.

Pie in the sky? Not in the least. With some fine tuning, we can hone the most important skills we will ever be called upon to use.

The power in these pages emerges from practices that nurture the development of empathy, of altruism, of conscience, of moral reasoning. Children in families—at least in North American families—where these practices are implemented have a clearer sense of right and wrong. They show more care for those around them. These children are what Diana Baumrind and others call *agentic*: they are more willing to stand up for and to act on their sense of right and wrong, and to act for the good of others and the community in general. Agentic children act not because of what they might gain, but from their sense that their actions further the common good.

The pages of this booklet bring us four decades of reseach that continues to refine our understanding of the power of good modeling, of teaching our children the *skills* of living in a democracy, of balancing high demands and a high level of nurturance, of understanding what belongs to the category of "morality" and what does not, and of understanding the concept and practice of what developmental psychologists call *induction*.

The Council for Spiritual and Ethical Education is fortunate to have five outstanding scholars contribute to this endeavor: five of the best known, most highly respected researchers and character education trainers in North America. Their words are thus, in all senses of the term, the words of the masters.

Authoritative Parenting

Diana Baumrind, who authored our first chapter here, is best known for defining four styles of parenting that today are generally accepted throughout a good part of the western world, and certainly in North America. What distinguishes one style from another is the degree to which parents are *demanding* (i.e., they set high expectations for their children's behaviors and require that their children live up to these expectations) and *responsive* (i.e., they are warm and supportive in their interactions with their children, and they are quick to respond when their children are in need).

When parents offer an appropriate balance of demands and nurturance—what Professor Baumrind refers to as *authoritative parenting*—they maximize the possibility of their children growing up

• with the courage to persevere when they face obstacles

• able to control their impulses

• being accountable to themselves and others

• with the drive to work toward goals that are both personally and socially desirable

• with an understanding of right and wrong; and

• with the tendency to choose right over wrong.

The last three characteristics in this list, when they are highly developed in children, represent what Diana Baumrind calls *optimal competence*. Such competence entails a balance of two semi-technical terms, *agency* and *communion*. The former is our ability and willingness to *act*: our ability to assert ourselves when we need to, to work to achieve our goals, to grow in our capacity to think and act independently, and to be self-regulating human beings.

The term *communion*, as might be expected, refers to that part of us that acts (that uses our *agency*) to work collaboratively with those around us in the service of others.

Like other contributors to this booklet, Baumrind addresses the issue of *power assertion*. Parents and other responsible adult figures must at times use their positions of authority to assert power. When one child is about to hurt another, we must do what we can to control behavior to prevent harm. However, there is a difference between asserting power through behavioral control and using psychological control.

Behavioral control is open and immediately understandable. Children understand when we grab and hold on to the arm that is swinging a stick, or when we send them to their rooms after three unsuccessful verbal attempts to get them to stop teasing a sibling. (We may even need to *put* them in their rooms if they refuse to comply with verbal demands). Children understand and respond appropriately to behavioral control, especially when the power assertion is accompanied by an explanation of why it is taking place and is later followed by helping the misbehaving child reconcile with the sibling. This is a point mentioned by a number of our authors.

Psychological control, on the other hand, tends to foster both anxiety and low self esteeem. Because it is not overt, children do not understand it and are frequently left confused about what it means. Psychological control entails actions like "guilt trips," or leading a child to believe that a parent's love is being withdrawn. Professor Baumrind points out that the most harmful form of psychological control is *wounding words*: words that belittle or demean the child. Wounding words are even more damaging to children than harsh physical punishment.

Modeling

It is no secret that being models of good behavior ourselves, and bringing good models into our homes—in person, but also via our use of media and our family discussions—is a powerful factor in our children's development. In his chapter on the subject, North America's best known character education trainer, Thomas Lickona, reminds us of several of ways that we can be, and offer, effective models for the children under our care.

First and foremost is the fact that our children are watching, and they are listening. They learn from both our actions and our words. They learn from us when we want them to, and when we do not want them to. They learn from the stories we tell, as well as from the comments we make about current events, about neighbors, about public figures, and about other family members. Children understand this as a moral issue. It is not negotiable.

The way we model commitment, restraint, generosity, and even anger influences our children's development. Is our anger dealt with openly and then left behind, or do we hold it tight and allow ourselves and others to suffer long after the anger's cause has subsided? Do we express our anger via its connection to an action, or do we seethe against the person who performed the action?

Practicing what we preach is an ancient admonition of tremendous importance. But Professor Lickona is often quoted for the corollary: that we should also *preach* what we practice. There is power in example. There is greater power when example is accompanied by direct teaching. Let us show our children what we stand for via our actions; but let us also tell them what we stand for and what our expectations are with our frequent and clearly expressed words.

Lickona reminds us of a number of insidious factors that, in addition to the many examples of true beauty, lie in some strands of our society's music, films and other media.

Finally, Professor Lickona stresses a fact that is recurrent in other sections of this booklet: the power in our modeling depends on the strength of our relationships. The more successful we are in showing our children that we respect, care for, and listen to them, the more they will look to us as models of values and virtues to develop.

Induction

In "Fostering Goodness, Teaching Parents to Facilitate Children's Moral Development," (see reference in chapter one) Professors Berkowitz and Grych referred to induction as "perhaps the single most powerful parental influence on children's moral development."

In short, induction is explaining reasons to children to help them understand both their actions and the actions' effects on others. Take the example of the 8-year-old who throws a pair of scissors across the room because her sister wants to use them. Some parents witnessing the event might respond with a quick slap: "I've told you not to do that!" Others might choose to assert power in some way, and perhaps to punish. Induction, in contrast, focuses less on the scissors thrower, and more on the act and the potential harm to someone else: "Madeleine, those scissors are sharp! You could have hurt Emily if they had hit her."

Induction is a useful process in both positive interactions and disciplinary situations. But because of the moral booster capabilities when it includes reintegrating a misbehaving child into the community (be this the family "community" or a playmate or group of playmates outside the home), we asked Marilyn Watson to address the practice by taking a special look at discipline strategies that foster social, emotional, and moral growth, while still curtailing misbehavior. Of course these strategies—like most discipline strategies—also minimize the chances of future misbehavior. However, the practices that Dr. Watson outlines recognize and build on children's innate needs for autonomy, competence, and belonging, and thus lead to more positive benefits than other strategies.

Berkowitz and Grych made their statement about the power of induction because, among the building blocks of character, induction seems to cover four important bases. It is linked to altruism in children, to growth in moral reasoning, to empathy, and to the development of conscience.

In disciplinary situations like the scissors incident described above, the ideal ending to the scene might entail Madeleine seeing if she can think of a way to repair whatever damage might have been done. Because the scissors did not hit her sister, no harm ensued and an apology may be sufficient. If they had hurt her, reparation might entail more than just an apology, and Madeleine's parent could help guide her through the process of learning to do so, or suggest some other appropriate actions. This helps develop Madeleine's repertoire of ways of reconciliation for her later life.

There are a number of reasons for induction's value. One is that induction links the self to the other ("Madeleine, you could have really hurt your sister!"). It helps develop empathy, it gives practice looking at events from another's perspective. Induction also helps develop moral reasoning: moral, because of its implications for others, and reasoning because it links causes to effects and helps the child in question understand that her actions affect—and could hurt—her sister. Furthermore, induction is effective because it contains both a cognitive component (knowledge: being aware of actions, effects, and reasons for actions) and an "affective" component: it teaches that others have feelings, but at the same time allows and encourages the development of the child's own feelings. The parent who is skilled in induction helps the child understand his or her feelings.

("I can tell that you were a little scared when you realized you almost hurt her. I'm glad you were aware of that.")

The many other ways of dealing with the scissors situation, two of which are mentioned above, might keep Madeleine from throwing scissors in the future. Harsh punishment might prevent futher actions, but the anger built up in the punished child may find its way out on a different child, outside the home. Similarly, asserting power by grabbing the scissors and forcing an apology may result in an unnecessary strain on the relationship between parent and child. Ways of addressing misbehavior that do not use induction's sympathetic focus on both children and an explanation of actions and how they affect others miss valuable opportunities to help children grow to be thoughtful, empathic, and caring.

Democratic Family Practices

Marvin W. Berkowitz points out that demonstrating respect for children to the extent that we bring them into family discussions and decisions as somewhat equal "partners" (the level of equality and participation depending on the developmental level of the child, of course) is essential if we want to train our children to be contributors to a democratic society; and it is also the right thing to do if we want to foster character growth—especially in regard to the concepts of justice and fairness. The *democratic respect* we show our children is, in itself, both justice (since they deserve respect) and an opportunity for us to *model* the kind of respect we hope they will show those around them as they continue to grow.

But respect is not sufficient, as Professor Berkowitz tells us. Both he and his colleagues in this booklet reiterate that, in addition to respecting our children, we need to communicate our respect with crystal clarity, we need to support them, and we need to make them *feel* loved. To be fully effective, our love entails helping our children believe that their voices are welcome and valued.

Believing that we welcome and value their voices happens best when we actively invite children to speak up and when, while they are speaking, it is clear to them that we are listening; we might even add an occasional challenging question, provided it is raised with that same tone of love and respect.

When we challenge our children in appropriate ways, the questions we pose stimulate moral reasoning: an important aspect of character growth. Although a certain amount of contention may be advantageous in peer discussions, children do not develop moral reasoning skills when discussions with parents are contentious. Grappling with concepts of right and wrong in a family setting is developmentally productive only when the child knows he or she is supported and cared about deeply.

Professor Berkowitz enriches his chapter with a number of practical suggestions: Socratic questioning, developing a mechanism for family problem solving, frequent check ins... and more. All are doable.

Domains of Social Reasoning

Professor Nucci's chapter about the domains of social reasoning is pertinent to parenting because three decades of research carried out across four continents is showing that "morality"—referring to issues and actions entailing fairness, justice, and human welfare—is indeed something that all cultures hold in common. Moreover, the way children around the world think about morality is relatively standard, whether they are growing up in India or Indiana, in Quebec or Qatar. As early as the age of four, children have a way of thinking about and judging moral actions that is different from the way they deal with issues of "convention." A five-year-old knows that it is never right to hit a smaller child or to keep all the candy for himself (moral issues); at the same time he, or she, knows that there are many other rules (conventional issues) which, albeit important, could be changed by a simple adult decision, like whether pajamas should be worn to school, or bathing suits to a birthday party, or shoes inside the house. Even a decision by a respected group of parents and teachers would not convince the average five-year-old that, beginning tomorrow, it is acceptable to push children off the swing and steal their bicycles.

Why is it important to understand what belongs to which domain? One reason is that children judge the competence of adults based on how we correct behaviors in the different domains. Fortunately, most of us do this appropriately, but research shows that addressing a moral infraction by reminding children that there are rules against such behaviors ("You know we are not allowed to hit others in this house!") is ineffective when it comes to fostering moral growth. Conversely, telling children how their actions affect others is frequently ineffective when the behavior in question belongs to the conventional domain ("Don't you know how that makes us feel when you wear a hat in the classroom?"), for it is in these latter cases that a reminder of the rules—ideally, along with their reasons—is the best approach to take.

Even more important, perhaps, is the fact that a number of parent-child disputes entail misunderstandings or differences of opinion regarding what belongs to one domain, and what belongs to another. An understanding of this can help resolve some, though certainly far from all, conflicts.

As is stated elsewhere in the text of our booklet, what works at home appears to be "best practice" for schools, also. Though less research has been done on these practices at school, preliminary evidence points very much in the same direction. Our hope, through this booklet, is that schools and parents will be able to work even more in tandem as educators, trainers, and nurturers for tomorrow's world.

This booklet was made possible through the contributions of a number of individuals. First and foremost, we are indebted to the authors who gave their time and talents to this publication. To one of them, Marvin W. Berkowitz, we are additionally grateful for two other reasons. Berkowitz and his colleague John Grych published their compelling article mentioned above, "Fostering Goodness," outlining the psychological and developmental bases of most of the practices described in this booklet. Their article was certainly influential on its conception. Professor Berkowitz was also helpful in recommending contributors for some sections of this booklet.

We are also tremendously indebted to David Weekley, whose vision and generosity made this work possible through financial support of an important character education initiative at CSEE, and through his wisdom in requesting that when schools participate in character initiatives, they include parents in their plans and the implementation of the plans. Not surprisingly, research is strong in its findings that when character education programs at school involve parents, they are more effective. Mr. Weekley was also helpful through his comments on the booklet as it was being prepared. This booklet is one attempt to help schools—since we hope that through them the power of the practices outined here will be passed on—help parents better understand the process of social, emotional, and moral growth (the growth of character) and how they can contribute to it.

A list of others who assisted in various ways with this booklet appears at the end. These individuals include parents of children from independent schools throughout the United States. A few of them are members of CSEE's Moral Development Team, a wonderful group of talented educators with whom the CSEE staff has had the opportunity to work and learn over the past three years.

There is, indeed, power in the pages that follow. We hope our pages are widely read, and that their advice is widely considered, widely practiced, and deeply effective. We have so much to gain with just a few adjustments.

David Streight
Executive Director
The Council for Spiritual and Ethical Education

High Demands, Great Support
Authoritative Parenting
In a Nutshell

In this chapter Diana Baumrind outlines four "styles" of parenting she first described four decades ago: unengaged, permissive, authoritarian and authoritative. After an extensive longitudinal study, Baumrind concluded that *authoritative parenting* is the style most effective in developing character and competence in children.

The children of authoritative parents tend to care more about those around them than their peers, they withstand peer pressure more easily, they face obstacles in their lives with greater persistence and success, and they engage more readily in service to others.

Authoritative parenting entails a balance of two characteristics:

• A high degree of *demandingness*. These parents have high expectations for their children's behavior, and they require that their children live up to these demands and expectations. Of course, the demands and expectations they set are developmentally appropriate and realistic in terms of their child's abilities.

• A high degree of *responsiveness* in the form of nurturance and support. Though they are demanding, authoritative parents only make demands that they feel their children can live up to, and they provide a high level of support as children strive to reach the high standards set for them. These parents express love, understand their children's needs for both protection and autonomy, and respond when they are needed.

Sometimes parents do need to assert their power to get children to comply with demands. Authoritative parents accompany such power assertion—which occasionally entails punishment of some sort—with reasons and explanations for their actions. This practice is called induction, and is outlined in Marilyn Watson's chapter and elsewhere in the booklet. Induction helps children develop moral reasoning skills.

Authoritative parents focus on constructive behavioral control, which is clear and aimed at creating compliance; they avoid using psychological control, which can be manipulative and wounding.

Authoritative parents praise their children for their good behavior and their laudable achievements. When behavior is substandard, they criticize what needs to be changed and, when necessary, they offer suggestions regarding improvements that might be made.

When done appropriately and for the right reasons, spanking or swatting of extremities does not appear to have the detrimental effects that some have stated it has.

Some definitions of terms useful to understanding authoritative parenting:

Agency relates to our ability and willingness to act. Children able and willing to act are described by professionals as being *agentic*.

Professor Baumrind and her colleagues refer to the children of authoritative parents as having the best chance of growing up *optimally competent*. One component of such children is their agency: these children are acting—taking increasing initiative—to be independent, autonomous young people learning to control their own actions and to be successful in their endeavors.

Communion is the companion characteristic of agency in optimum competence. Communion refers to our awareness of, and concern for, others. Children who are *communal* are concerned about those around them and collaborate with them toward common goals.

Authoritative Parenting for Character and Competence
by Diana Baumrind

The way parents exert authority over their children directly affects the development of character and competence (Baumrind, 1996; Steinberg, 2001). *Character* is the aspect of personality that relates to accountability, persistence in the face of obstacles, and control of impulses. *Competence*, broadly defined, helps us reach personally, and socially, desired goals. Competence to know right from wrong, and to regulate our actions in choosing right rather than wrong, is what marks the human species as "the ethical animal" (Waddington, 1960).

Optimum competence requires a balance of what psychologists call *agency* (see Bakan, 1966) and *communion*. *Agency* is self-oriented: it is our drive to achieve independence, individuality, and self-aggrandizement, and is measured by the extent to which we are self-regulated, autonomous, achievement-oriented, and assertive. *Communion* is other-oriented: it is our drive to be of service to others and to engage collaboratively with them. We are *communal* when our interactions with others are prosocial and cooperative. The most competent children—those we refer to as "optimally competent"—have balanced these qualities. When agency is uncurbed by communion, children tend to have a selfish disregard for the needs of others (e.g., the six-year-old who excludes his three-year old sister from play). Such a deficiency eventually invites reciprocated harm. When communion is not tempered by agency, children tend to be self-effacing, compliant, and susceptible to the negative influences of others (e.g., the teenager who drinks and drives because "everyone else does.").

Patterns of Parental Authority

In 1960 I initiated research to investigate how childrearing patterns affect children's development of character and competence (Baumrind, 1967, 1971, 1991a). More than 100 parents and their children participated in my longitudinal study of childrearing practices and their effects when the children were in preschool, middle school, and high school. At each stage trained psychologists spent some fifty hours studying the characteristics of members in each family, and their interactions. One team observed parent-child interactions both at home and in the laboratory, and then interviewed parents about these interactions. A second team observed each child's interactions with peers in school and on the playground; the children were interviewed when they were in middle school and high school.

The parents in our study demonstrated qualitatively different approaches to how they balanced demandingness and responsiveness. *Demandingness* refers to the way parents use power; it is how they monitor and supervise their children's activities, and how they control, prohibit, and modify children's behaviors to fit their standards. *Responsiveness* refers to how parents express love, balance their children's needs for protection and autonomy, and comply with their children's needs and wishes.

We discovered that children's levels of competence and adjustment could be explained by how parents integrated responsive and demanding practices. Four primary parenting patterns emerged, which I labeled unengaged, permissive, authoritarian, and authoritative. These parenting patterns and associated child outcomes are described in detail in two articles in the references at the end of this chapter (Baumrind, 1991a, 1991b). Although both authoritative and authoritarian styles of parental authority are highly demanding, their ways of asserting power differ markedly, as do the effects on their children's development of character and competence.

Unengaged Parents

Unengaged parents are neither demanding nor responsive. They discourage dependency, and contribute little in the way of governance or education to their child's development of character or competence. They are uninvolved because they want to remain unencumbered by childrearing responsibilities. Some are detached and neglectful whereas others are more actively rejecting and cold. The

> *"Adolescents with unengaged parents had the lowest achievemet scores and suffered the most from anxiety, depression, and substance abuse"*

majority of children with unengaged parents were neither agentic nor communal. No primary school child from an unengaged home was optimally competent. Adolescents with unengaged parents had the lowest achievement scores and suffered most from anxiety, depression, and substance abuse.

Permissive Parents

Permissive parents are undemanding, but responsive. They do not require mature and competent behavior. They set few explicit clear standards, limits, or prohibitions that would require their children to behave responsibly and respect the needs of others. They do not consistently enforce basic rules for conduct such as respect for others' needs, property, and feelings. These parents give their children wide latitude to govern their own behavior, and fail to provide adequate structure and stability to their children's lives. While they could demand mature behavior, prohibit undesirable behavior, and obtain compliance, they more frequently indulge their children or rely on psychological manipulation by bribing, withdrawing love, or making the child feel guilty for hurting the parent. When children resist or test limits, permissive parents avoid confrontation in an effort to be perceived as good friends rather than authority figures. Children raised permissively were not self-regulated, prosocial, or achievement-oriented; during adolescence, these children were more likely to abuse drugs than were children whose parents were more demanding. The parents' indiscriminate acquiescence to children's demands tended to foster dependency rather than responsible self-sufficiency.

> *"... parents' indiscriminate acquiescence to demands tended to foster dependency... rather than self-sufficiency"*

Authoritarian Parents

In contrast to permissive parents, *authoritarian* parents are demanding, but unresponsive. They lack warmth, tenderness, and show little concern for their child's perspective, They tend to be disapproving and hypercritical, rarely praising their child's constructive achievements (like timely completion of chores or good grades) or encouraging initiative. They micromanage their child's activities and impose unreasonable regulations based on parental whims. They schedule activities without considering conflicts with their child's plans. Authoritarian parents make no effort to communicate the reasons for their directives or sanctions. To get their children to behave, and to preserve their hierarchical authority, they use threats, punishment, criticism, guilt induction, and bribes rather than explanation, negotiation, or reason. Authoritarian parents impose consequences for disobedience that are harsh, incoherent, and sometimes unpredictable. Their demands are arbitrary, immoderate, inconsistent, and developmentally inappropriate, such as expecting quiet for long periods from a preschooler. They insist on conformity to parental wishes in rigid and inflexible ways, as opposed to being realistic, issue-oriented and guided by the reality of the child's interests, abilities, and needs. Children perceive authoritarian parents as unapproachable, and their parents' use of power as arbitrary. The children of authoritarian parents in our study gave in to peer pressure, had poorer academic skills, and experienced greater rates of anxiety and depression than their peers.

> *"The children of authoritarian parents... gave in to peer pressure, had poorer academic skills, and experienced greater rates of anxiety and depression..."*

Authoritative Parents

Authoritative parents are both demanding and responsive. By contrast to both permissive and authoritarian parents, authoritative parents integrate and balance high levels of responsiveness with high levels of demandingness in ways that are beneficial to children's development. By contrast with authoritarian parents, authoritative parents encourage individuality and independence; they are warm and understanding of their child's perspective. Authoritative parents require mature behavior within the child's range of ability, and base demands and prohibitions on their child's attributes, abilities and developmental level. When they make power assertive demands, they accompany their demands with explanations to help the child understand the parent's conception of appropriate behavior. These parents use reason and discussion to obtain compliance and are willing to negotiate when they deem their child's objections to be reasonable. They praise worthy behavior and achievement, and criticize actions that require change. Their sanctions connect logically to the consequences of their child's actions. They monitor children's activities and know their whereabouts.

> *"... children of authoritative parents were both more community oriented and more agentic..."*

Because authoritative parents are warm, responsive, and autonomy-supportive as well as power-assertive their children are motivated to restore family harmony by complying or else by constructively dissenting in an effort to change their parent's mind rather than to defiantly or evasively disobey. Children of authoritative parents were both more community-oriented and agentic than their peers.

Authoritative versus Authoritarian Forms of Power Assertion

Parents' right to exercise authority in ways that restrict children's freedom features prominently in the antithetical worldviews of American liberals and conservatives. George Lakoff (1996) employs the metaphors *Strict Father* and *Nurturant Parent* to capture how fundamental differences in Americans' worldviews are reflected in their childrearing practices. Strict Father conservatives, representing the stabilizing force in society, uphold restraint, hierarchical order, tradition and permanence. Consistent with their Strict Father belief that filial piety symbolizes God's authority, evangelical counselors such as Rosemond (1994) and Dobson (1992) advise parents to compel children, by punishment—physical when necessary—to submit their will to adult authority (Ellison & Sherkat, 1993). Limitations and restrictions are based on hierarchy in which parents are dominant and children are subordinate.

From Strict Father's perspective the lenient practices advocated by Benjamin Spock's 1946 *Common Sense Book of Baby and Child Care* fuel a youth culture subversive to traditional values. Nurturant Parent liberals, representing the transformative force in society, uphold freedom, equality, novelty and change. They foster mutually responsive communication among family members so that children will choose to follow parents' leadership motivated by love and respect, not fear of punishment.

> *"... words that demean or belittle the child... [are an] even more potent contributor to children's maladjustment than harsh physical punishment"*

Parents vary in the extent to which they acknowledge the unequal balance of power in the family. By virtue of physical size, experience and control of resources, parents can usually enforce their wishes despite a child's resistance; children cannot do likewise. In early childhood, power legitimates parents' rights to exercise authority. There are important differences, however, in the way authoritarian and authoritative parents use power, and these contribute to differences in their children's competence and character. As the adolescent becomes increasingly capable of thinking abstractly (Piaget's [1965] formal operational thought) and thus of either legitimating parental authority or arguing against it on principle, they increasingly consider authoritarian forms of power assertion to be illegitimate, and thus they put up resistance.

Although both authoritarian and authoritative parents use behavioral control, authoritarian parents, unlike authoritative parents, also use psychological control, coercive power, wounding words, and harsh physical punishment to manage their children. *Behavioral control* is overt, confrontive, and aimed at inducing compliance with parents' directives, whereas *psychological control* is covert, intrusive, and aimed at manipulating the child's psychological world and personal identity by such indirect methods as guilt-induction and threats of loss of love which bypass the child's conscious will. Psychological control, unlike behavioral control, fosters anxiety and low self-esteem (Barber, 2002). *Coercive power* is inflexible, repressive, and leaves no room for discussion. In response to the superfluous threat to their freedom, children tend to resist coercive power (Brehm, 1993). *Wounding words* (Teicher, Samson, Polcari, & McGreenery, 2006) that demean or belittle the child have been shown to be a prevalent and even more potent contributor to children's maladjustment than harsh physical punishment (Bugental & Happaney, 2000; Straus & Field, 2003).

Physical Punishment and Spanking

The use of physical punishment remains hotly contested. When punishment is used correctly, a more desirable pattern of behavior is taught and reinforced, and contingencies are clear and consistent. In such cases, punishment can effectively deter a young child's disruptive behavior (Patterson, 1997). Punishment, both physical and verbal, is aversive to most parents, however, as it is to the child. One influential review (Gershoff, 2002) concluded that although physical punishment can ensure short-term compliance, its negative side-effects—such as increased antisocial behavior—outweigh its benefits. However, Gershoff's review has been criticized (e.g. Baumrind, Larzelere, & Cowan, 2002) for its reliance on retrospective recall and cross-sectional correlations that cannot separate children's effects on parents from parents' effects on children (for example, did physical punishment cause a child to behave aggressively, or was the child's aggressive behavior the reason why the parent spanked?).

The most serious deficiency of Gershoff's review is its failure to distinguish between the effects of "spanking" and those of harsh or abusive physical punishment. By *spanking* we refer to physical punishment that is within the normal range and is "a) physically non-injurious; b) intended to modify behavior; and c) administered with an opened hand to the extremities or buttocks" (Friedman & Schonberg, 1996, p. 853). Unlike wounding words or harsh physical punishment, spanking appears to be an unlikely cause of detrimental outcomes, given that 79% to 97% of American children have been spanked as toddlers (Straus & Stewart, 1999), and psychopathology is relatively uncommon.

> *... authoritative parents phased out [spanking] as the child approached adolescence*

Larzelere and Kuhn (2005) concluded from their comprehensive review of the literature that in contrast to the negative side-effects of physical abuse, and possible negative effects of spanking on older children, effects of spanking on 2- to 12-year-old children are benign and similar to effects of other common corrective interventions such as timeout and verbal reprimands. Authoritative parents in my study were at the median in their use of physical punishment with preschoolers, but phased out this form of punishment as the child approached adolescence. Authoritarian parents, however, met noncompliance with harsh punishment, both physical and verbal.

Reciprocal Rights and Responsibilities of Parents and Children

The cornerstone of all ethical systems is the moral norm of reciprocity, represented in Christian religion by the Golden Rule, and in Buddhist thinking as karma, or the sum of the ethical consequences of one's actions (Baumrind, 1980). *Reciprocity* refers to a balanced relationship in which each party has both rights and obligations. The subordinate norm of *complementarity* states that one's rights are the other's obligation. The reciprocal relationship between the rights and obligations of parent and child constitutes the basis of Rousseau's' social contract, which he defined as follows:

> The most ancient of all societies, and the only one that is natural, is the family: and even so the children remain attached to the father only as long as they need him for their preservation. As soon as this need ceases, the natural bond is dissolved. The children, released from the obedience they owed to the father, and the father, released from the care he owed his children, return equally to independence. (Rousseau, 1767)

Applied to the parent-child relationship, reciprocity implies balance between the rights and duties of parents and children; if children have a right to be nurtured, then their caregivers have a complementary obligation to nurture. Parental authority comes from fulfilling the moral obligation parents owe their children to nurture them from birth to maturity. Children have responsibilities relative to their nurturance rights, which include the obligation to comply with parental directives and to return their love. By requiring their child to accommodate the needs of others—by sharing, complying and tending to chores—while committing themselves unconditionally to their child's well-being, authoritative parents demonstrate the beneficial effects of the principle of reciprocity. Exploitation by authoritarian parents, or indulgence by permissive parents, or neglect by unengaged parents interferes with children's learning the norm of reciprocity and acknowledgement that their actions have consequences for the self and others. Permissive proponents of liberation rights for children (e.g. Farson, 1974; Kohn, 2005; Neill, 1964) negate the principle of reciprocity by simultaneously claiming that, because of their temporary dependence, children are entitled to beneficent protection, but because of their inherent status as autonomous persons children have an equal right with adults to self-determination.

If respect for persons signifies respect for what they truly are, then respect for children requires that their dependent and immature status be recognized. To the extent that children are dependent they are entitled to unconditional commitment from adult caretakers and are reciprocally obliged to respect the authority of their parents. This means that children may not claim the full rights to self-determination appropriate to an independent person; parents may, and should, oversee their children's education, and censor their media exposure, friends, and attire. As they approach adolescence, however, children gradually relinquish the privileges of dependent status and assume the responsibilities and entitlements of adult status consistent with their developing capabilities.

Variants of Authoritative Parenting

Although the four major patterns of authority (authoritative, authoritarian, permissive, disengaged) we identified are best known, we identified two variants of the authoritative pattern when the children were older (Baumrind, 1991c). We called these variants "democratic" and "directive." Democratic parents were just as responsive, and just as supportive of autonomy as authoritative parents, but they were somewhat less demanding. Directive parents were as demanding but somewhat less responsive and autonomy-supportive than authoritative parents. On our continuous conservative-versus-liberal measure, democratic parents were more liberal, and directive parents were more conservative, than authoritative parents who were at the mean. Although the democratic pattern has not, to my knowledge, been identified in other cultural groups, the directive pattern has been described in Asian and Afro-American cultures in the United States.

In Asian cultures, concern and love are typically manifested by firm control and strict governance. Chao (2000) described an indigenous form of Chinese parenting, which she refers to as "training" or "governance" entailing parental involvement and firm control, which she reports is associated with achievement and self-esteem. Chao interpreted training as authoritarian-like, and therefore concluded that in the Chinese context authoritarian parenting could have beneficial effects. In my view, however, training is more like authoritative than authoritarian parenting because parents' purpose in training, according to Chao, is to assure harmonious relations with others and the welfare of the family unit, and to advance the child's long-term interests, rather than to dominate and restrict the child, as is the case for authoritarian parents.

Similarly, Afro-American parents are frequently described as authoritarian, because they tend to manifest higher levels of restrictive control than middle-class Anglo-American parents. However, as McLoyd (1990) and others state, the reason why many concerned parents in high-risk environments physically enforce immediate obedience and restrict their children's activities is to protect their children from harm rather than to maintain hierarchy and suppress dissent. In high-risk—but not in low-risk—neighborhoods, restrictive control has been found to foster desirable attributes such as good grades (Gonzales, Cauce, Friedman, and Mason, 1996).

Unlike authoritarian parents, directive parents do not lack real warmth, and they are well-meaning and caring rather than hurtful and domineering. Asian training style and the restrictive style imposed in dangerous neighborhoods by Afro-American parents are not intended to, and apparently do not, undermine children's autonomy, but instead foster culturally-valued forms of competence. Therefore, rather than conclude that authoritarian upbringing is adaptive in non-Anglo cultures, I conclude that these indigenous Asian and Afro-American parenting styles are better classified as directive than authoritarian.

Conclusion

Although my classification system was conceived specifically for the purpose of differentiating among children who were raised in middle-class Anglo families rather than to uncover a universal family typology, authoritative and authoritative-like styles of leadership have been found to foster optimal competence in both

> *"authoritative... styles of leadership have been found to foster optimal competence in both school and home settings"*

school (Pellerin, 2005; Wentzel, 2002) and home settings for diverse cultural groups (Baumrind & Thompson, 2002; Smetana, 2005; Sorkhabi, 2005; Steinberg, 2001).

On the other hand, authoritarian and permissive parenting styles both minimize opportunities for children to learn how to cope with stress and frustration. They do this either by curtailing children's initiative (in the case of authoritarian parents) or by giving children free rein (as permissive parents do) (Baumrind, 1973). Democratic and directive variants of authoritative parenting are almost as successful, whereas unengaged parents who are neither responsive nor demanding, and authoritarian and permissive parents who are either disproportionately demanding or responsive, fail to foster children's development of character and competence in any cultural context.

References

Bakan, D. (1966). *The duality of human existence: Isolation and communion in Western man.* Boston, MA: Beacon Press.

Barber, B. K. (2002). *Intrusive Parenting: How psychological control affects children and adolescents.* Washington, DC: American Psychological Association.

Baumrind, D. (1967). Child care practices anteceding three patterns of preschool behavior. *Genetic Psychology Monographs,* 75(1), 43-88.

Baumrind, D. (1971). Current patterns of parental authority. *Developmental Psychology Monograph,* 4 (1, Pt. 2), 1-103.

Baumrind, D. (1973). The development of instrumental competence through socialization. In A. Pick (Ed.), *Minnesota symposia on child psychology* (Vol. 7, pp. 3-46). Minneapolis: University of Minnesota Press.

Baumrind, D. (1980). The principle of reciprocity: The development of prosocial behavior in children. *Educational Perspectives,* 19(4), 3-9.

Baumrind, D. (1991a). The influence of parenting style on adolescent competence and substance abuse. *Journal of Early Adolescence,* 11(1), 56-95.

Baumrind, D. (1991b). Parenting styles and adolescent development. In

R. Lerner, A. C. Petersen, & J. Brooks-Gunn (Eds.), *The encyclopedia on adolescence* (pp. 758-772). New York: Garland.

Baumrind, D. (1991c). Effective parenting during the early adolescent transition. In P. E. Cowan & E. M. Hetherington (Eds.), *Advances in family research* (pp. 111-163). Hillsdale, NJ: Erlbaum.

Baumrind, D. (1996). The discipline controversy revisited. *Family Relations, 45*(4), 405-414.

Baumrind, D., Larzelere, R. E., & Cowan, P. (2002). Ordinary physical punishment: Is it harmful? Comment on Gershoff (2002). *Psychological Bulletin,* 128(4), 580-589.

Baumrind, D., & Thompson, R. A. (2002). The ethics of parenting. In M. Bornstein (Ed.), *The handbook of parenting* (2nd ed., Vol. V, pp. 3-34). Mahwah, NJ: Lawrence Erlbaum.

Brehm, J. W. (1993). Control, its loss, and psychological reactance. In G. Weary, F. H. Gleicher, & K. L. Marsh (Eds.), *Control motivation and social cognition.* New York: Springer-Verlag.

Bugental, D. B., & Happaney, K. (2000). Parent-child interaction as a power contest. *Journal of Applied Developmental Psychology, 21*(3), 267-282.

Chao, R. (2000). The parenting of immigrant Chinese and European American mothers: Relations between parenting styles, socialization goals, and parental practices. *Journal of Applied Developmental Psychology,* 21(2), 233-248.

Dobson, J. (1992). *The new dare to discipline.* Wheaton, IL: Tyndale House.

Ellison, C. G. & Sherkat, D. E. (1993). Conservative Protestantism and support for corporal punishment. *American Sociological Review, 58*, 131-144.

Farson, R. (1974). *Birthrights.* New York: Macmillan.

Friedman, S. & Schonberg, S. K. (1996). The short-and long-term consequences of corporal punishment. Supplement to *Pediatrics, 98*, 857-858. American Academy of Pediatrics.

Gershoff, E.T. (2002). Parental corporal punishment and associated child behaviors and experiences: A meta-analytic and theoretical review.

Psychological Bulletin, 128(4), 539-579.

Gonzales, N.A., Cauce, A.M., Friedman, R.J., & Mason, C.A. (1996). Family, peer, and neighborhood influences on academic achievement among African-American adolescents: One-year prospective effects. *American Journal of Community Psychology, 24*(3), 365-387.

Kohn, A. (2005). *Unconditional parenting: Moving from rewards and punishments to love and reason.* New York, NY: Atria Books.

Lakoff, G. (1996). *Moral politics: What conservatives know that liberals don't.* Chicago: University of Chicago Press.

Larzelere, R. E., & Kuhn, B. R. (2005). Comparing child outcomes of physical punishment and alternative disciplinary tactics: A meta-analysis. *Clinical Child and Family Psychology Review, 8,* 1-37.

McLoyd, V. C. (1990). The impact of economic hardship on Black families and children: Psychological distress, parenting and socioemotional development. *Child Development, 61,* 311-346.

Neill, A. S. (1964). *Summerhill.* New York: Hart.

Patterson, G. R. (1997). Performance models for parenting: A social interactional perspective. In J. Grusec & L. Kuczynski (Eds.), *The handbook of parenting and the transmission of values.* New York: John Wiley & Sons.

Pellerin, L. A. (2005). Applying Baumrind's parenting typology to high schools: Toward a middle-range theory of authoritative socialization. *Social Science Research, 35,* 283-303.

Piaget, J. (1965). *The moral judgment of the child.* London: Routledge & Kegan Paul. (Original work published 1932)

Rosemond, J.K. (1994). *To spank or not to spank.* Kansas City, MO: Andrews & McMeel.

Rousseau, J. J. (1952). *The social contract.* University of Chicago: Great Books, Encyclopedia Britannica. (Original work published 1767).

Smetana, J. G. (2005). Adolescent-parent conflict: Resistance and subversion as developmental process. In L. Nucci (Ed.), *Conflict, contradiction, and contrarian elements in moral development and education* (pp. 69-91). Mahwah, NJ: Lawrence Erlbaum.

Sorkhabi, N. (2005). Applicability of Baumrind's parent typology to collective cultures: Analysis of cultural explanations of parent socialization effects. *International Journal of Behavioral Development, 29,* 552-563.

Spock, B. (1946). *Common Sense Book of Baby and Child Care.* New York: Duell, Sloan and Pearce.

Steinberg, L. (2001). We know some things: Parent-adolescent relationships in retrospect and prospect. *Journal of Research on Adolescence, 11*(1), 1-19.

Straus, M. A., & Field, C. J. (2003). Psychological aggression by American parents: National data on prevalence, chronicity, and severity. *Journal of Marriage and Family, 65(*4), 795-808.

Straus, M. A., & Stewart, J. H. (1999). Corporal punishment by American parents: National data on prevalence, chronicity, severity, and duration, in relation to child, and family characteristics. *Clinical Child and Family Psychology Review, 2,* 55-70.

Teicher, M. H., Samson, J. A., Polcari, A., & McGreenery, C. E. (2006). Sticks, stones, and hurtful words: relative effects of various forms of childhood maltreatment. *The American Journal of Psychiatry, 163*(6), 993-1000.

Waddington, C. H. (1960). *The ethical animal.* Chicago: University of Chicago Press.

Wentzel, K. R. (2002). Are effective teachers like good parents? Teaching styles and student adjustment in early adolescence. *Child Development, 73,* 287-301.

The Power of Modeling
In a Nutshell

Loving children, respecting children, setting high standards for children are essentials. But there is more. Our children are aware of
• how we treat one another as spouses
• how we treat other adults in our homes and outside
• how we talk about others in the presence of our children

Our children note the moral stands we take:
• do they see us, and hear us, take stands for values we hold dear?
• do they see us take stands against issues counter to our values?

Questions to consider
Do we bring positive models, in person, into the home?
Are our friends positive models for our children?

Do we bring positive models into the home, in other ways?
Do the TV shows we watch, the books we read, the magazines we subscribe to tell our children about the values we want them to learn?

Is our behavior consistent?
Do our children see us practicing what we preach?
Do our children hear us preaching what we want them to practice?

Do our children hear our moral reasoning—our explanations of why we think the way we do?
When we express our admiration of moral models or situations, do we also explain why we admire the individuals involved?
When we express disapproval, do our children understand why?

Do we act to reduce the negative models in our lives?
Do we control (especially for younger children) or monitor the films they see, the games they play, the TV shows they watch, the places they go?

The stronger our relationships, the more powerful we are as models.
Our children should see us as human. They should understand that *our* "character," too, is a work in progress. We, too, stumble but are still trying.

The Power of Modeling in Children's Character Development
by Tom Lickona

The character education movement of the past two decades, arguably the most important educational reform movement of our time, reflects a deepening national concern about character. I encounter this concern wherever I go. At an independent school where I was to give a talk to parents, one of the host mothers said, "I worry about the effects of all the material affluence that surrounds our kids. Will they come to value it above everything else?"

The lessons of history remind us that riches do in fact tend to corrupt. The educator James Stenson, author of *Compass: A Handbook on Parent Leadership* (2003), points out that today most of us are rich when measured by the standards of the past. We enjoy a level of prosperity—an abundance of food, drink, amusements, clothing, and technological devices— unprecedented in human history.

But are our children better off? Many, to be sure, possess a resilient spirit and admirable character, but all too many have a poorly formed conscience, are weighed down by self-centeredness, and lack a sense of purpose. It is children from the higher socioeconomic levels, Stenson notes, not the children of the poor, who are the most likely to commit suicide.

Some young people are wise enough to perceive and reject the spiritual emptiness of much of modern life. In his book, *With Love and Prayers: A Headmaster Speaks to the Next Generation* (2000), Father Tony Jarvis, the Episcopal priest who led Boston's Roxbury Latin School for boys for thirty years, quotes a recent Roxbury graduate:

I see so many people just going through the motions: Get into a good school, so you can get into a good college, so you can get a good job, so you can get a better job, so you can get rich and die.

In one of his daily "character talks" to the boys at Roxbury—this talk aimed at getting them to think about what life goals are worth pursuing— Father Jarvis shared a story about a childhood friend:

This guy had everything—good looks, a brilliant mind, a winning personality. He was a schoolboy athletic hero, went to the best college, married a gorgeous—and nice—wife, climbed speedily to the top in business, made a bundle of money, bought an estate in the suburbs, had three kids, a dog, a cat, a lawn service, and three cars. The perfect model of success. My sister just saw him at a high school reunion. He had just up and left it all—his estate, his wife, his family—and he was talking about quitting his job.

He said: "You remember what I was like as a kid? I knew what I wanted—the whole package of success. I knew I'd be happy if I realized that dream. But when I got it, it turned to dust. I just got sick of it all."

"Each of us," Father Jarvis says, "is engaged in a lifelong search for a life worth living." Today's media-driven culture, with its worship of money, sex, status, and power, can easily lead our children in wrong directions. As parents and teachers, we must do all we can to help them develop a long-term vision of what really makes for a meaningful and fulfilling life.

For starters, we can share with them the important finding that cultures around the world affirm three life goals as sources of authentic happiness: (1) maturity of character—becoming the best person we can be; (2) loving relationships such as marriage, family, and friendships (religious believers would include a relationship with God), and (3) making a positive difference in the lives of others (Devine et al., 2000). Developing good character is at the heart of all three of these pursuits. What can we do to help our children to develop the strengths of character that will set them on the path to a productive, ethical, and fulfilling life?

> *"It has to do with how we treat each other a spouses—something that our children have literally thousands of opportunities to observe"*

"They Set a Good Example"

In hundreds of interviews with parents, young adults, and others, I've asked people, "What did your parents do to try to teach you good values and good character?" People speak of many things, including their parents' love, their high expectations, their firm discipline, and their wisdom about life. But far and away, the most common answer I receive is simply, "My parents set a good example."

However, there's much more to teaching by example than meets the eye. It involves treating our children with love and respect, but it goes well beyond that. It has to do with how we treat each other as spouses—something that our children have literally thousands of opportunities to observe. Our marital behaviors, we can be sure, will imprint themselves on their moral memories. When we fight, do we fight fair? Do we use disrespectful and denigrating language, or do we maintain in our words and tone a basic respect, even in the heat of an argument? Do we forgive and reconcile soon after, or hold on to our anger and resentment? Healthy families, research shows, commonly have reconciliation rituals that enable them to forgive and make up quickly (Curran, 1985).

The example we set includes how we talk about others—relatives, friends, neighbors, and teachers. The mother who says "That's a dumb homework assignment," is modeling a disrespect for the teacher that will not be lost on the child. "Disrespect," says one parent educator, "usually begins in low-level ways. Kids become desensitized to it."

Our modeling also includes all the ways we manifest concern for the welfare of others outside our family. One father I interviewed remembered his parents' ethic of service:

The thing that sticks in my mind is an atmosphere of genuine concern for others outside the home. My father was a volunteer fireman and rescue worker and still is, in his sixties. My mother was always a volunteer of some sort and was always helping out others in the community. They were generous to others, even when they had little for themselves. Many people would praise my parents to me and my siblings because of their kindness.

Another vitally important dimension of our example consists of the moral stands we take—especially stands that are unpopular with our children or at odds with what other parents are permitting. What do we prohibit? Violent video games? TV shows and movies that contain sex, violence, or foul language? All forms of pornography? Music with lyrics that denigrate particular groups? Immodest dress? Parties where there's drinking? Prom overnights? Said a father at an independent school: "Our daughter is the only one among her friends who is not going to the overnight beach party after the senior prom. She is very unhappy with us right now, but that's our decision."

Do our kids know where we stand on the moral issues of our times—abortion, war and peace, threats to the environment, the plight of the poor? If we've ever taken a stand in the workplace or public arena or even in a conversation with one other person, have we shared that with our children? Stands like these define our values. They let our children know what we care deeply about and are willing to take risks for. That's essential if we hope to pass on our values and convey the importance of integrity and courage in a life of character. If our children never see us standing up for what we believe, never going against the tide, how can we expect them to have the courage to stand up to pressure from their peers?

Exposing Kids to Other Positive Models

We increase the power of our own example when we expose our children to other positive role models. This can be as simple as having someone to dinner who is a good person and then drawing out that individual's thoughts and experiences. Children enjoy and benefit from listening to thoughtful adult conversation.

Friends are obviously important. Peers are powerful role models. We should talk with our kids about what a true friend is and share our own experiences with friendships. (Indeed, sharing experiences from our youth will help kids understand us as persons and parents, and these stories will often reverberate throughout their lives at each stage of maturity.) We can send them to schools where there is a culture of character—of doing your best work and doing the right thing. We can encourage them to join a good club or youth group where they will have a chance to meet other kids who share their interests and values.

We can also take our children out into the community to witness, and be part of, the good that others do. Australian educator Andrew Mullins, in his book *Parenting for Character* (2005), recounts what one father did to teach his 15-year-old compassion for others:

> The son was badgering him to buy him yet another pair of $200 Nikes. The father said, "Come on mate, let's go out for dinner." He took him into the city, and they stood together in the queue of a soup kitchen. Now, two years later, one night each week, the son helps run the soup kitchen.

Several things no doubt contributed to the effectiveness of what this father did. He set an example of compassionate concern himself. He exposed his son to less fortunate persons that his son might otherwise never have met. He gave him the opportunity to experience the joy of serving others, arguably the best antidote to the self-centeredness that can take over in adolescence. At the same time, he exposed his son to the collective good example of all the other kind-hearted people who were working in that soup kitchen week after week.

Examples of good role models abound if we take the trouble to find them. Somewhere in the evening paper there's at least one story of integrity, courage, or compassion. (The examples of bad character—the latest sports scandal, corruption in high places, violations of human rights—are also valuable learning opportunities.) The Giraffe Heroes Project (www.giraffe.org) has developed a bank of more than 1,000 stories of everyday heroes of all ages who have shown compassion and courage by sticking out their necks for others. The website www.teachwithmovies.com catalogues hundreds of good films that offer positive role models and strong character themes, such as "A Man for All Seasons" (integrity), "Gandhi" (the power of non-violence), "Chariots of Fire" (fidelity to principle), "Spitfire Grill" (sacrificial love), "Chronicles of Narnia" (loyalty and courage), and "Amazing Grace" (justice, faith, and perseverance).

Biographies of moral and spiritual giants such as Mother Teresa, Viktor Frankl, Harriet Tubman, and William Wilberforce can inspire all of us to be more than we might otherwise be. There are hundreds of fictional stories, from picture books to novels, whose admirable characters will live in a young person's heart and imagination (see *Books That Build Character* (1994) by William Kilpatrick for an extensive annotated bibliography). Finally, there are enjoyable books that are full of wisdom about life, such as Hal Urban's *Life's Greatest Lessons* ((2004) and Sean Covey's *The Six Most Important Decisions You'll Ever Make* (2006). (Covey's includes lots of stories from the lives of teens showing how to make good decisions about school, family relationships, friends, drugs and alcohol, and sex.)

Preaching What We Practice

If we want our example to have maximum impact, our kids need to know the values and beliefs that lie behind it. We need to practice what we preach, but we also need to preach what we practice.

Research points to the power of combining example with direct teaching. Character is "caught" *and* taught. Samuel and Pearl Oliner's *The Altruistic Personality* study (1988) interviewed 406 persons who rescued Jews from the Nazi Holocaust and 126 people who had lived in the same parts of Nazi-occupied Europe but did *not* get involved. Compared to non-rescuers, rescuers were much more likely to say that their parents both modeled and explicitly taught good values. For example, rescuers' parents were much more likely to teach an attitude of tolerance toward other cultures and religions. One man said: "My father taught us to love God and neighbor, regardless of race or religion. At my grandfather's house, if a Jew happened to drop in when we were reading the Bible, he would ask him to take a seat."

Modeling Moral Reasoning

Setting a good example includes sharing our deepest values and beliefs—teaching *what* we think is right and good—but also includes explaining *why* we think the way we do. Modeling good moral reasoning is an important, and sometimes neglected, part of the example we set.

Consider a moral issue that concerns nearly every secondary school in America: cheating. In *Smart & Good High Schools* (Lickona & Davidson, 2005), our two-year study of what award-winning high schools are doing to foster eight essential strengths of character, we identify the rise of cheating as one of the major moral challenges facing schools and society. For a sobering picture of the widespread erosion of integrity, read David Callahan's *The Cheating Culture: Why More Americans Are Doing Wrong to Get Ahead* (2004). An estimated half of resumes now contain lies. Duke University's Center for Academic Integrity, in its survey of more than 18,000 students at 61 U.S. high schools, found that 76% admitted to cheating. The data show a steady increase in cheating over the past several decades, accompanied by the growing attitude that cheating is the way the world works (McCabe, 2001). One high school student said, "Politicians cheat, businessmen cheat, athletes cheat—why not students?"

If we want young people to resist the temptation to join the cheating culture, they will need clear moral reasons why cheating is wrong. Here are four:

1. Cheating is unfair to all the people who aren't cheating.

2. Cheating is a lie, because it deceives others.

3. Cheating violates trust and damages relationships.

4. Cheating will corrupt your character. If you're dishonest now, you'll find it easier to be dishonest later in life—on the job and perhaps even in your closest relationships.

We also want our children to understand that they will lose self-respect if they cheat and that they will never be able to be proud of anything they got by cheating. We want them to believe what may seem very hard to believe at first: that it is better *not* to get ahead than to do so by cheating. We want them to have honesty at the core of their moral identity so they would feel "out of character" if they were ever to cheat. Indeed, that's what

> *"Our children also need memorable examples of principled moral reasoning in the face of often intense pressure to go along with what others are don't"*

one independent school found to be the ethical orientation of its most morally mature upper school students. A small percentage of students at each grade level, interviewed as part of a study of cheating, said things like, "I could never cheat—it's not who I am." We want all young people to think like that.

Our children also need memorable examples of principled moral reasoning in the face of often intense pressure to go along with what others are doing. The torture and sexual humiliation of prisoners in Iraq, Afghanistan, and elsewhere would have been less likely to occur if even a few onlookers had objected. A compelling exception to silence in the face of evil comes from the My Lai incident in Vietnam. When Lt. William Calley gave his soldiers the order to shoot—resulting in the massacre of more than 300 Vietnamese villagers—there was one soldier who disobeyed the order. His name was Michael Bernhardt. We should share with our kids his moral reasoning:

I can hardly do anything if I know it's wrong. The law is only the law, and many times it's wrong. It's not necessarily just, simply because it's the law. My kind of citizen would be guided by his own laws. These would be more strict, in a lot of cases, than the actual laws (Scharf, 1978).

Bernhardt is saying that just because something is legal or approved by authority doesn't mean it's right. There is a higher law to which we are all accountable, namely, the moral law. That's the essence of what the Nuremberg trial judges told the Nazi concentration camp commanders when they said those officers were "just following orders."

Or consider a domain of decision-making where young people often demonstrate their lowest levels of moral judgment and self-control: sex. This is an area where parents often go mute, either because they're not clear about their own thinking, would just as soon not know what their kids are doing, or are afraid their teenage son or daughter will ask, "Did *you* have sex when you were my age?" An appropriate response to that question is, "Whatever mistakes I did or didn't make when I was growing up are not the point. The way to make the best life for yourself, a life without regrets, is to make the best possible decisions—ones that will help you avoid getting hurt and avoid hurting others."

In today's debased sexual culture, young people very much need to hear, from people they love and respect, intelligent reasons why they should save sexual intimacy for a truly committed love relationship. Parents can turn for help to authors who have made a well-reasoned case for waiting. Here, for example, is an excerpt from a pamphlet titled "Love Waits":

Love is patient; love is kind. Love wants what is best for another person. Love will never cross the line between what's right and wrong. It's wrong to put one another in danger of having to deal with hard choices, choices that could change your lives forever.

Having sex before marriage may feel right for the moment. But the possible costs of an unexpected pregnancy, abortion, and sexually transmitted disease—as well as the deep hurts that can come from a broken relationship—outweigh the feelings of the moment. The feelings are temporary; their consequences are long-lasting.

All good things are worth waiting for. Waiting until marriage to have sex is a mature decision to control your desires. If you are getting to know someone—or are in a relationship—remember: If it's love, love waits.

We can also take heart from a finding from the National Longitudinal Study of Adolescent Health (Resnick et al., 1997): When parents communicate their disapproval of teen sex, their children are more likely to delay sexual involvement.

Reducing the Influence of Negative Examples

Wise parents will seek to maximize their children's exposure to good example. But especially in today's toxic popular culture, they will also strive to reduce their children's exposure to bad example.

Unfortunately, all too many parents have lowered their vigilance. According to *Kids and the Media at the New Millennium*, a Kaiser Family Foundation study (1999), two-thirds of American children between 8 and 13 have their own TVs in their bedrooms. Counting all forms of electronic media, youth between 8 and 18 consume, on average, 6 hours and 43 minutes of electronic media a day.

The Internet has brought new dangers. A 2000 Netvalue Report on Minors found that U.S. youth under 17 spent 65% more time on adult pornography Internet sites than they did on game sites. Four of the ten who had visited a pornographic site were girls. Pamela Paul, author of *Pornified: How Pornography is Transforming Our Lives, Our Relationships, and Our Families* (2005), quoted a female porn star who was on tour in England promoting her best-selling memoir and who was surprised that pre-teen girls were showing up at signings (Secor, 2006).

> *"Teaching media literacy... is somethig else both schools and families can do to reduce the impact of unhealthy media content"*

Reducing the destructive impact of negative media starts with our clear and authoritative guidelines. Many parents have found it helpful to sit down with their kids and say something like:

Use of all media in our home is a privilege, not a right. That privilege must be exercised with our approval and our presence—and in a way that is consistent with our values as a family. So for any particular TV show, DVD, video game, or website, here's the question: Is it consistent with what we value and believe as a family?

Despite our best efforts, however, our kids will inevitably be exposed to at least some aspects of negative media. Teaching media literacy, the skills of critically analyzing media messages—Who created this message? For what purpose? What values are being conveyed? What attention-getting techniques are being used?—is something else both schools and families can do to reduce the impact of unhealthy media content (see Lickona & Davidson, 2005, for teaching strategies and supporting research).

The Stronger Our Relationship, the Greater Our Influence

Our influence as role models is embedded within a host of interacting factors. The impact of our example on our children depends, for example, on the quality of our relationship. The stronger our relationship, the greater our positive impact.

> *"... teens who were relatively mature in ther reasonng rated ther fathers as much warmer and more involved with them..."*

Research bears this out. One parenting study (Holstein, 1972) compared "successful fathers" (who had themselves reached Kohlberg's stage of principled moral reasoning and whose 13-year-old children had reached a stage of moral reasoning mature for their age, where they showed concern about doing what was right in the eyes of parents and teachers) with "unsuccessful fathers" (principled themselves but whose 13-year-olds were at a less mature, more self-centered stage of reasoning). This study found that teens who were relatively mature in their reasoning rated their fathers as much warmer and more involved with them than did teens with relatively immature reasoning.

In developing a close relationship with our children, there is no substitute for spending time with them. As most of us have experienced, there is a special intimacy to one-on-one time. One of my favorite examples of this comes from the autobiography of Christian Barnard (1974), originator of the heart transplant:

> Whenever we were ill, my father got up late at night to doctor us. I suffered from festering toenails that pained so much I would cry in bed. My father used to draw out the fester with a poultice made of milk and bread crumbs or Sunlight soap and sugar. And when I had a cold, he would rub my chest with Vicks and cover it with a red flannel cloth. Sunday afternoons we walked together to the top of the hill by the dam. Once there, we would sit on a rock and look down at the town below

us. Then I would tell my problems to my father, and he would speak of his to me.

Modeling Commitment

There is no more powerful example, certainly none that children feel more deeply, than how we model a commitment to providing a loving and stable family for them to grow up in.

About a million children see their parents divorce each year. Divorce is a sensitive subject. Marriages fail for all kinds of reasons, including child abuse, spousal violence, and infidelity. Researcher Judith Wallerstein's *The Unexpected Legacy of Divorce: A 25-Year Landmark Study* (2000) documents the often lasting repercussions of family breakdown for both kids and adults. For a great many children, time does not heal the wounds. As young adults, many of them fear commitment, and if they do marry, often panic in the face of the first marital fight—because they have no templates for solving conflicts.

"The most important thing parents can do for their children," said one mother, "is to love each other and stay together." If we can manage to hold our marriages and families together in good times and bad, we will teach our children a profound life lesson about the meaning of commitment.

Modeling Faith in Something Larger Than Ourselves

The 2002 research report, "Religious Involvement and Children's Well-Being" (www.childtrends.org), finds that youth who frequently attend religious services and say their faith is important to them exhibit higher levels of altruism and lower levels of drug and alcohol use and sexual activity. It is certainly possible to be an ethical person without being religious, and having religious faith by no means guarantees that a person will be good. But for many persons, including many young people, religion gives life a higher meaning and an ultimate reason for leading a good life.

> *"... religion—or any other world view that places a high value on doing good—has a better chance of taking root in a child's conscience and character if it is central to our own"*

Clearly, religion—or any other world view that places a high value on doing good—has a better chance of taking root in a child's conscience and character if it is central in our own. We can't give what we haven't got. Mary, a young mother who is devout in her own faith, recalls her father:

> Dad always closes his letters with, "Work hard and pray a lot." This never sounds phony because it's what he does. He has worked hard all his life. He built the two homes we lived in and did all the repairs. And he prays throughout the day. My most powerful image of my father is of catching him kneeling at the foot of his bed, late at night before he retired, saying his personal prayers.

I once asked a mother I knew to be serious about the practice of her faith, "What values or heritage do you hope to pass on to your children that you don't expect them to get from school?" She answered:

> Faith in God. The value of an interior life. Prayer. A religious view of the universe. I would like them to view the world and everything in it—creation, people, events—through the lens of faith because I believe that's the most freeing way of seeing things, with the greatest potential for happiness, direction, and peace.

I then asked her, "How does your faith translate into what you teach your children about morality?" She said:

> If you see God as the center of things, it affects everything. It affects why you behave in certain ways and not others. There is a standard of behavior. It comes partly from people who have tried to discern the mind of God over the ages. We also have our own hearts to listen to. There is someone who has created us to behave in a certain way—so much so that if we don't behave in that way, we are unhappy, we create problems for ourselves. We are called to goodness, to live our lives according to a very high standard.

I asked how this vision is made concrete in the life of the family She spoke of weekly worship and daily prayer. God, she said, is part of everyday conversation, about matters ranging from why you shouldn't be mean to your little brother to saving sex for marriage. Then she described a tradition the family had recently begun, inspired by a sermon on world hunger. On the first night of each week, they have a "fasting dinner"—usually a piece of fruit for the children and a cup of broth for the parents. The meal begins with a prayer written by the oldest child, age 10:

> Lord, we pray for all the hungry people in the world, that they may

become well and fed, and that the pain they suffer will be lifted from their hearts—and that all people will turn their hearts to generosity and compassion.

> *"The money saved by not having a regular dinner is put into a jar and sent to a charity to relieve world hunger and poverty"*

The money saved by not having a regular dinner is put into a jar and sent to a charity working to relieve world hunger and poverty. Sometimes, at the meal, the mother or father will read a letter from the charity reporting progress in relieving a crisis in one part of the world or the outbreak of a new crisis somewhere else. Says the mother, "It helps us to be aware of how much suffering there is and to enter into that in a small way. We want our kids to know that God calls us to love our neighbor, wherever our neighbor is, and that we are all members of the same human family." Such traditions, and the beliefs that motivate them, ground character development in a meaning system, a view of life and our relations with each other in which doing the right thing and being a good person are of central importance.

Whatever one's world view, our children need a spiritual rudder in their quest for character. They need a vision that addresses life's largest questions: What is the meaning of life? What is the purpose of *my* life? How can I make my life count for good?

Especially as they enter adolescence, when doubts and questioning are a normal part of intellectual development, our children should know that the spiritual life is often full of struggle, even dark nights of the soul. *Time* magazine's September 3, 2007 cover story reports a new book (Kolodiejchuk, 2007), consisting largely of Mother Teresa's letters to her spiritual directors, revealing that she spent almost 50 years in a state of deep spiritual pain because of what she experienced as the withdrawal of God's presence. And yet she never abandoned her faith or wavered in carrying out what she believed was God's mission for her: to care for the poorest of the poor.

Dealing with Moral Failure

Biblical wisdom tells us that "the just man falls seven times a day." On some days, for many of us, it may feel more like seventy. Moral failure is an inescapable part of trying to live a good life.

We can model how to deal with this, too. Our kids should know that we see our own character as a work in progress, just as theirs is. We should humbly seek their forgiveness when we treat them badly. We should teach them that being faithful to our standards and ideals does not mean never failing, but rising every time we fall. And as we go about the challenging work of trying to be good role models, we can take consolation from what a wise bishop once said: "Our children don't need to see parents who are perfect, but only ones who are trying."

References

Barnard, C. (1974). Selections from *One Life*. In J.L. Milgram & D. J. Sciarra (Eds.), *Childhood revisited*. New York: Macmillan.

Callahan, D. (2004). *The cheating culture*. New York: Harcourt.

Covey, S. (2006). *The 6 most important decisions you'll ever make*. New York: Fireside.

Curran, D. (1985). *Stress and the healthy family*. Minneapolis: Winston Press.

Devine, T., et al. (2000). *Cultivating heart and character*. Chapel Hill, NC: Character Development Group.

Hostein, C. (1972). The relation of children's moral judgment level to that of their parents and to communication patterns in the family. In R.C. Smart (Eds.), *Readings in child development and relationships*. New York: Macmillan.

Jarvis, F. Washington. (2003) *With love and prayers*. Boston: David Godine Publishers.

Kids and media at the new millennium. (1999). Kaiser Family Foundation.
Kilpatrick, W. (1994). *Books that build character*. New York: Touchstone.
Kolodiejchuk, B. (2007). *Mother Teresa: Come be my light*. New York: Doubleday.

Lickona, T. and Davidson, M. (2005). *Smart & good high schools: Integrating excellence and ethics for success in school, work, and beyond*. New York: Center for the 4th and 5th Rs. Available at www..cortland.edu/

character

McCabe, D. (2001). Cheating: Why students do it and how we can help them stop. American Educator (Winter).

Mullins, A. (2005). *Parenting for Character*. Lane Cove, Australia: Finch Press.

Oliner, S. and P. (1988). *The Altruistic Personality*. New York: The Free Press.

Paul, P. (2005). *Pornified. How Pornography is Transforming Our Lives, Our Relationships, and Our Families* Henry Holt & Company.

Resnick, M.D., et al. (1997). Protecting adolescents from harm: Findings from the National Longitudinal Study of Adolescent Health, *Journal of the American Medical Association*, 278.

Secor, S. (2006). A culture adrift. *Morality in media* (March).

Scharf, P. (1978). *Moral education*. Davis, CA: Responsible Action Press. Stenson, J. (2003). *Compass: A handbook on parent leadership*. New York: Scepter.

Wallerstein, J., J. Lewis & S. Blakeslee (2000). *The unexpected legacy of divorce*. (Hyperion)

Urban, H. (2004). *Life's greatest lessons*. New York: Simon & Schuster.

Induction and Discipline for Character
In a Nutshell

Induction is perhaps the most powerful parent practice outlined in this booklet. This becomes obvious in part from the number of authors who mention it. Induction entails bringing the child's attention to an action, focusing on the action's effect on another person and pointing out the cause-and-effect relationship. In positive situations, for example, it might look like mom bringing Susan's attention to how pleased their neighbor was because Susan took their puppy back after it escaped. In cases of misbehavior, the process is similar: "Matthew, look at how sad Billy is. The name you called him really hurt his feelings." Induction in disciplinary situations becomes even more powerful when the misbehaving child has the opportunity (and is encouraged, but not forced) to repair the "damage" done. In the Matthew/Billy interaction, the adult in question might say "I wonder if you could think of some way to make him feel better."

What happens in many disciplinary situations is that Matthew is punished. He may or may not make fun of Billy again, but if he does not make fun again, it is because of fear of punishment rather than out of sensitivity to a peer.

• Punishment often leads children to feel sorry for themselves, rather than to appropriate guilt for actions or to empathic responses to others.

• Sometimes we need to assert our power to control children's behaviors or to stop actions from happening. When such is the case:

  • Helping children focus on another's distress, and helping children think of ways to relieve that distress, makes it easier to keep the power assertion in the background.

  • Providing children with explanations for our use of power both models good character and helps them develop control over their actions.

Children are naturally inclined to want to develop warm and trusting relationships with us; they also naturally inclined to cooperate with us.

When warm and trusting relationships are built, most of their interactions will entail cooperation.

• When children do not cooperate with us, it is usually because they lack an understanding of the situation or because they lack certain skills. If this is the case, they are best helped by explanations and by our teaching them the necessary skills.

• Punishment is sometimes needed. The less we resort to it, the more effective we are; it is best used after, or in conjuction with, the other "tools" of developmental discipline: explanations or observations about a situation that children may not have seen, reasons why certain actions are more or less beneficial than others, instruction in skills, reminders of appropriate behaviors.

• Self-interest is *not* the primary motivator for children. Though self-interest is a factor, children are much more strongly motivated by their love for us and by their desire to be accepted by the group.

• By temperament, some children are more difficult to deal with than others. These children, even more than others, need our teaching, our explanations, our patience and our support.

• All children have needs for autonomy, competence, and belonging.

• We can foster autonomy by giving children choices. Even young children can be given choices, but they might handle choices between two possibilities more effectively ("Do you want the yellow one or the red one?") than an overwhelming array of options ("What color do you want?").

Discipline Strategies
That Support Character Growth
by Marilyn Watson

Discipline, the actions we take to get our children to do what we want them to do—or to stop doing what we don't want them to do— is pervasive in parenting. Researchers have estimated that parents of children between the ages of two and ten engage in some kind of disciplinary interaction about every six to nine minutes (Hoffman, 2000). Of course, many of these disciplinary interactions are little more than directions, "Stop playing with your cars on the table," "Please share the dolls." However, there are lots of occasions when our children's behavior requires more than a simple direction. On such occasions we need to take more control of the situation. Several studies have shown that how we exercise this control can profoundly affect our children's character development. Parental discipline strategies that are low in power assertion and involve instruction and empathy induction (a focus on the harm the child has caused to others) relate positively to children's concern for others and a general prosocial orientation. On the other hand, a heavy emphasis on power assertion and punishment are related to higher levels of aggression and antisocial behavior (Hoffman, 2000; Hoffman & Saltzstein, 1967; Peck & Havighurst, 1960; Zahn-Waxler, Radke-Yarrow, & King, 1979). However, as parents we frequently feel the need to exercise power in order to keep our children safe and to assure that they are well behaved.

So, what specifically does discipline that is low in power assertion and effective in fostering character look like? First, let's review what it means to be moral. In a nutshell, a moral person is someone who wants to be good, fair, and caring and who usually acts in moral ways for moral reasons or feelings. A moral reason can be as simple as a belief that it's not nice to hurt others; a moral feeling can be as simple as feeling sorry for someone or a wish to comfort or make another happy. Actions taken to avoid punishment or receive a reward, even if they are morally right, are not moral actions. Because moral action requires moral reasons or feelings, it makes sense to stress moral reasons and feelings (rather than rewards and punishments) in our disciplinary interactions.

Focus on Moral Reasons or Feelings

When our children's actions cause or are about to cause harm to another, we can foster their moral growth by helping them understand the other's situation or by focusing them on the other's unhappiness. Seeing the pain they have caused will usually lead children, on their own, to respond empathically and feel bad about their hurtful actions. On the other hand, punishments, such as removing a toy, sending children to time out, spanking, or distancing ourselves, are more apt to cause children to feel sorry for themselves, and thus block an empathic response and the feeling of moral guilt, both of which are building blocks of mature morality.

> *"punishments... are more apt to cause children to feel sorry for themselves, and thus block an empathic response..."*

Helping our children understand and empathize with the feelings of the person harmed, whether that be an aunt who has brought an undesirable birthday present, a younger brother who has been excluded from play, or a parent whose book has been carelessly ripped, underscores the very basis of morality—that it's not good to harm others. Often, we can go one step further in supporting moral development. We can help our children repair, at least to some extent, the harm they have done.

Although they may need time to regain their composure, it's surprising how eager children can be to engage in some reparative act, once they realize the harm they have caused. Sometimes a heartfelt "I'm sorry" is all that's possible. A child cannot repair Grandma's broken vase or undo the disappointment they showed at Aunt Mary's birthday present. However, especially as they get older, children frequently can find a way to undo or at least ameliorate the harm they caused. A torn book can be taped; a shunned younger brother can be invited into the play; Aunt Mary can be given a hug; and a drawing of the vase can help Grandma feel better. Of course, parental power assertion is usually involved to gain the child's attention and stop the misbehavior. However, focusing on the natural inclination to respond empathically to another's distress—helping them think of ways to relieve that distress, while refraining from punishing—keeps that power assertion in the background.

When we help our children feel empathy for those whom they have harmed we do not have to *make* them repair the harm, they will *want* to do so. Because everyone makes mistakes and causes harm, when we help our children make reparation, we build their intrinsic moral motivation, teach them the skills involved in reparation, and show them how people of character respond when they cause harm.

Offer Explanations

Many common disciplinary situations don't involve clear harm to another. For example, saying 'no' to a child who wants to go out to play in the rain, refusing to let a ten-year-old child go to a movie rated PG 13, insisting that our children say 'please' and 'thank-you' or insisting that they practice the musical instrument they have chosen to learn, or clear their plates and clean their rooms, do not obviously involve harm to others.

Sometimes we find ourselves in a conflict with our children because we are trying to protect them. For example, we may fear that they will do poorly in school if they don't do their homework. Sometimes we say 'no' because we judge that what the child wants will make demands on us that are too high given the small benefit the child will receive. A father who has just finished washing the floors may rightfully be loath to allow his child out to play in the mud. Sometimes we want to teach our children to share in family responsibilities, so we arbitrarily choose the task of clearing their plate from the table as the place to begin. Sometimes we simply place a high value on politeness or cleanliness.

> *"Whatever our reasons may be for controlling aspects of our chidren's behavior, explaining... is a way both to model moral action and to achieve control with limited power assertion"*

Whatever our reasons may be for controlling aspects of our children's behavior, explaining them to our children is a way both to model moral action and to achieve control with limited power assertion. "Because I said so" is pure power assertion. Threatening punishment or offering a reward simply ratchets up the power. Giving an explanation,

> *"Our children won't always accept our explanations. They may whine, beg, or stomp off in anger. Still, we have given them an honest explanation."*

on the other hand, provides a model of moral behavior. By explaining the reasons for our decisions or actions we are showing respect for the personhood of our children. A core aspect of morality involves taking others seriously as persons and treating them as we would like to be treated (Tigner, 1999).

Our children won't always accept our explanations. They may whine, beg, or stomp off in anger. Still, we have given an honest explanation. We can hold to our decision hoping that someday they will understand. As long as we do not find ourselves constantly saying 'no' or constantly having to push our children toward behaviors they are reluctant to perform, our explanations will usually suffice. Even if our children do not agree with our reasons, once they have learned to trust that we care about them, they will usually comply, at least in so far as they are able (Hoffman, 2000; Nucci, 2001). Because they are still developing their skills, we may need to provide a little help. For example, the father who doesn't allow his child to play outside in the mud may need to help the child find an engaging indoor activity; the parent whose child balks at room cleaning may need to work with the child to break down the task or help with parts of it. We may need to teach our children skills we take for granted, such as perseverance and organization.

Focus On Teaching Social, Emotional, and Moral Skills and Understandings

Our children are born with powerful dispositions to attach to us, and to imitate us, their primary caregivers. They are also born with a capacity for empathy. They want to cooperate and please us and to care about the welfare of others, even though their momentary wants and self-interests can compete with their desire to please us or to respond empathically toward others. If left unchecked, their self-interest can result in disobedient and selfish behavior. But being moral is not about being selfless; it is about knowing how to balance the needs and wants of the self with the needs and wants of others. This learning takes time.

Developmental psychologists have documented many social, emotional, and moral skills and understandings that children need to learn as they mature and experience life. Throughout their childhood years, children are learning and relearning these skills. For example, they need to learn to trust us and to balance their need for independence with our need to teach and keep them safe. They need to learn to regulate and control their emotions, to accurately communicate their feelings and thoughts, to understand the feelings and situations of others, to negotiate and compromise, and to set goals and monitor their own behavior. They also need to learn and to see the moral issues involved in common situations such as playground teasing and taking other's things.

> *"... they often fail to behave as we want them to because they lack one or more of these skills and understandings."*

There are a huge number of social, emotional, and moral skills and understandings that our children need to learn in order to succeed at doing the right thing. Whether our children are two or twelve, they often fail to behave as we want them to because they lack one or more of these skills and understandings. The best time to teach a skill is when it is needed. When, in response to our children's misbehaviors, we focus on teaching a skill that might have helped them behave better rather than punish or order them to stop misbehaving, the control we exercise is less about the assertion of power and more about helping them achieve success. What our children experience is not so much our control of their behavior (although we have exercised considerable control), but our help as they try to control their own behavior.

Let me illustrate this approach to discipline with a family story involving a temper tantrum. Several years ago, when Caitlin, our granddaughter, was two-years-old, my husband and I decided to take a picnic and visit a winery near our daughter's house. Since our daughter was home with Caitlin and a new baby, we decided to see if Caitlin would like to come with us on our picnic. Caitlin was very excited and did indeed want to go on a picnic with Grandma and Grandpa. However, as I went to lift Caitlin into her car seat she began to scream, sob, and thrash about. I had no idea what I did to cause her to be upset, but there was no doubting that she was very upset. Our daughter, after trying to calm her down while standing beside the car, eventually swooped Caitlin up and carried her inside. My husband and I sat in the car unsure of what to do. However, we believed that Caitlin really did want to come with us and that if we left she would be very unhappy. So, we sat and waited.

After a while our daughter came back outside with Caitlin in tow. Caitlin was now calm, a little subdued, but quite clear that she wanted to come with us. This time I let my daughter put Caitlin in the car and off we went. At first Caitlin was quiet and we drove along in silence. However, after some minutes had passed we heard a very small voice saying, "You can tell people your sad feelings. You can tell them your happy feelings too."

Let's examine this story from the perspective of discipline focused on teaching needed skills. Like many two-year-olds, Caitlin had difficulty regulating her emotions, particularly her negative emotions. Once she started crying and kicking she was powerless to stop on her own. By removing her to a less charged place, holding her close, and talking in a quiet, calm voice, our daughter was able to help Caitlin get control of her emotions and calm down. Although our daughter exercised considerable power in this incident, the power she used was power to help Caitlin gain control of her emotions. When children perceive their parent's control as aimed at supporting or helping them, they are far less likely to resent the control (Baldwin, Baldwin, & Cole, 1990, Pitkanen-Pulkkinen, 1980).

Once Caitlin was calm, her mother continued with more "instruction" in social and emotional skills and understanding. She helped Caitlin see that if she was unhappy with something someone did she could just tell the person. This was the first of many lessons Caitlin would receive about communicating feelings with words and trusting that others will hear her and respond with care. And even though Caitlin would need many more such lessons, it's clear that she had heard this initial instruction and was working on understanding it. I chose to describe this small, almost insignificant incident with Caitlin because it so clearly demonstrates the striving to learn that is in all our children. It also suggests what could have gone wrong if we had used our adult power to force Caitlin into the car without giving her time with her mother.

Contrary to such folk wisdom as "give them an inch and they'll take a yard," our children love us and want to please us. As annoying as they can seem sometimes, our children want to be good. Of course they are motivated by strong self-interests, we all are, but self-interest is neither the only nor the most prominent of their motivations. The idea that children are predominantly motivated by self-interest and thus must be controlled by appealing to that self-interest through rewards and punishments is unsupported by research. Social and developmental psychologists have documented that children are motivated by their love for us, by a desire to be part of a community and to learn and master the skills valued by that

> *"... children are motivated by their love for us, by a desire to be part of a community and to learn and master the skills valued by that community"*

community, and by a desire to control their own behavior (Stayton, Hogan, & Ainsworth, 1971; Deci & Ryan, 1985; Sroufe, 1996; Pianta, 1999). When they fail to do the right thing it is more likely because they lack needed social and emotional skills, or don't fully understand the situation.

Discipline as Parent/Child Collaboration

The discipline strategies associated with children's positive moral development—providing explanations and moral reasons; inducing empathy; teaching social, emotional, and moral skills; and avoiding punishment—are essentially collaborative strategies. But this is collaboration between unequal partners. We are more competent than our children. We need to accept more responsibility for the outcome as we guide them in the collaborative process. However, as parents, we lead busy lives with many tasks to accomplish and limited time. Also, our children have strongly felt needs of their own and have undeveloped social and emotional skills. Several factors can make it difficult to achieve, at least at times, a collaborative approach to discipline with our children.

Temperament and Time

Sometimes we just don't have the time, at least at the moment, to explain, teach, or guide our child toward compliance. Also, some children have temperaments that lead them to require lots of intervention and patience. For example, temperamentally bold children manage to get into many potentially troublesome situations so that monitoring them in respectful ways can be exhausting. Some children are emotionally more volatile than others, and helping these children regulate their emotions can sometimes require more time and patience than we have. There will be occasions when we lose our patience, cut explanations short and simply take control. Reminding ourselves, over and over, that our children want to be good and need our help to succeed can usually increase our patience and bolster our efforts to provide reasons and explanations, even if hours or days later.

Children's Autonomy Needs

The combination of children's needs for autonomy and their relatively undeveloped judgment and social and emotional skills often leads to problems. As parents we must exercise control for our children's safety, as well as their and our well being. While this control can conflict with our children's autonomy needs, we can lessen this conflict by relinquishing some control in areas where it is not absolutely necessary that our child comply perfectly. Does it really matter if our child finishes every green bean on the plate, wears matching socks, or stops playing right this instant? When it really does matter, we usually can provide some measure of autonomy by offering choices that still result in compliance. Would you like to write your thank-you note to Aunt Mary tonight after supper or tomorrow morning? You really hurt your brother's feelings. What would you like to do to help him feel better?

> *"A powerful way to provide for autonomy and achieve a solution to our children's unacceptable behavior is to engage them in trying to solve the problem"*

A powerful way to provide for autonomy and achieve a solution to our children's unacceptable behavior is to engage them in trying to solve the problem. Of course this only works if the child sees our problem as a problem. Because they care about us they often will see the problem if we explain it. Their solutions, however, may sometimes be unorthodox.

Anyone who has ever been a parent has found it a problem to get their children ready for school in the morning. I have been to workshops where presenters seriously suggested that parents let their children go to school in pajamas, and I have known parents who have yelled and pleaded and finally resorted to removing toys in order to motivate their child to dress more quickly. Alfie Kohn, a prominent educator and author, describes in his wonderful book, *Unconditional Parenting,* what happened in his house when he and his wife decided to ask their preschool daughter to think of a way to solve this problem.

> Not long after our first child started preschool, my wife and I fell into the trap of nagging and relying on various coercive strategies. What we were doing in an increasingly desperate effort to get her going in the morning was tiresome for all of us, and we weren't acting like the parents we wanted to be. Finally, we sat down with our daughter at a time when none of us was feeling pressured, and calmly laid out the problem. Then, instead of lecturing, we listened. ...we brainstormed together: What could we do that would make mornings more pleasant for all of us?

> Abigail suggested that things might go a lot faster if she could just sleep in the clothes she was going to wear the following day. We couldn't think of any good reason not to try this, so we did....It worked. Mornings are still a struggle sometimes, but less so than if getting dressed were still part of the routine. (From *Unconditional Parenting* by Alfie Kohn, pp. 174-175)

Our Beliefs About Children

To engage our children in collaborative problem solving or to take the time to figure out how to help them behave better, we have to trust that our children want to please us and want to be good. Deeply imbedded in our culture is the belief that children are primarily self-interested and will be spoiled if we do not punish their inconsiderate, selfish, or troublesome actions. Because children lack many of the skills and understandings needed to behave well, their behavior frequently can be annoying. Annoying behavior coupled with a belief that children are essentially self-interested can easily result in anger and a belief that punishment is necessary and justified. Reminding ourselves, when confronted with our children's misbehaviors, that our children want to please us, want to have friendly peer relations, want to learn, and want to be part of their community, may help us find collaborative discipline strategies likely to support their moral growth.

Absolute Power Can Corrupt

As parents we have enormous control over our children's lives. It may not be as much as we'd like in this age of media bombardment, but still we control their resources, schedules, level of personal freedom, and security. With such power we can sometimes be seduced into using it for our own advantage.

Because we have the power to demand compliance, we do not have to listen to our children's reasons or consider their point of view, or even explain the reasons behind our demands. Because we have the power to give our own needs more weight than our children's, our decisions do not have to be fair. Of course our needs are important and should be considered, but it can be tempting to give our needs more importance just because we can. Our power allows us, and can sometimes seduce us, to behave disrespectfully or unfairly toward our children. It's likely our children will notice.

On the positive side, when we take the time to explain or teach, when we temper our use of power in favor of working with our children toward a mutually acceptable solution, we are providing a powerful moral example to our children. We are living the central moral message that the possession of power does not entitle one to disregard the needs, wants, and rights of less powerful others.

The Good Enough Parent

Borrowing a phrase from D. W. Winnicott, we do not have to be perfect to be good enough to positively support our children's moral development. As outlined above, there are lots of factors that might interfere with our succeeding in taking a collaborative approach in any given disciplinary interaction. There will be times when we are too rushed and hassled, and times when we can't figure out what skill our child is lacking, and times when our anger overcomes our kindness, and times when we just lose our patience. However, as long as our overall disciplinary interactions are collaborative, we will succeed in helping our children build strong moral selves.

Summary

Discipline strategies likely to support children's moral development rely less on power assertion, stressing instead explanation and moral reasons and feelings, and providing support for moral behavior by teaching social, emotional, and moral skills and understandings. Discipline approaches that incorporate these characteristics have come to be known as Developmental Discipline. It is *developmental* because they are guided by what we know about children's developmental needs and tasks and because they hold a view of children as biologically predisposed to respond empathically, to learn, and to form strong attachment bonds with their parents. Although our children's self-interest will sometimes overwhelm their more positive instincts, current research supports the view that our children want to be good and want to cooperate with us. Our task, as our children's moral socializers, is thus best construed as *helping* our children learn to act morally and build strong moral selves rather than as *making* them do so.

"Discipline strategies likely to support children's moral development rely less on power assertion"

Developmental Discipline is a collaborative approach to discipline and is thus different from many common discipline approaches. For some, good discipline is primarily a set of tools for controlling children's behavior. Those who view discipline in this way usually assume that children are basically self-interested and that effective discipline is a matter of showing children that good behavior is rewarded while bad behavior is punished.

Discipline approaches that rely on dispensing rewards or punishments are based in views of children's motivations and needs that research has shown to be inadequate. Although they are consistent with deep cultural beliefs about children, and they work (for a time at least) to control children's behavior, the behavioral control is achieved at a moral cost. While parents must exercise their power in discipline situations, approaches that focus on control of children's behavior through the dispensing of positive and negative consequences tend to lead children to be angry and fearful. In the long run, they lead to children becoming oppositional, displaying less prosocial and more antisocial behavior (Hoffman, 2000).

In contrast, collaborative discipline approaches that limit power assertion by stressing explanation, moral reasons and feelings, and by teaching social, emotional, and moral skills and understandings, help our children strengthen their ability and their desire to lead good, ethical lives.

References

Baldwin, A. L., Baldwin, C., & Cole, R. E. (1990). Stress-resistant families and stress-resistant children. In J. Rolf, A. S. Masten, D. Cicchetti, K. H. Nuechterlein, & S. Weintraub (Eds.), *Risk and protective factors in the development of psychopathology* (pp/ 257-280). New York: Cambridge University Press.

Deci, E. L., Ryan, R. M. (1985). *Intrinsic Motivation and Self-Determination in Human Behavior.* New York: Plenum Press.

Hoffman, M. L. (2000). *Empathy and moral development: Implications for caring and justice.* New York: Cambridge University Press.

Hoffman, M. L. & Saltzstein, H. D. (1967). Parent discipline and the child's moral development. *Journal of personality and social psychology,* 5, 45-57.

Kohn, A. (2005). *Unconditional parenting: Moving from rewards and punishments to love and reason.* New York: Atria Books.

Nucci, L. P. (2001). *Education in the moral domain.* New York: Cambridge University Press.

Peck, R. F., & Havighurst, R. J. (1960). *The psychology of character development.* New York: John Wiley & Sons.

Pianta, R. C. (1999). *Enhancing Relationships Between Children and Teachers.* Washington, DC: American Psychological Association.

Pitkanen-Pulkkinen, L. (1980). The child in the family. *Nordisk psykologi,* 32 (2), 147-157.

Sroufe, L. A. (1996). *Emotional development: The organization of emotional life in the early years.* New York: Cambridge University Press.

Stayton, D.J., Hogan, R., & Ainsworth, M.D.S. (1971). Infant obedience and maternal behavior: The origins of socialization reconsidered. *Child development.* 42, 1057-1069.

Tigner, S. S. (1999). A seven-point program. In K. Ryan & K. E. Bohlin, *Building character in schools.* San Francisco: Jossey-Bass, 193-205.

Zahn-Waxler, C., Radke-Yarrow, M., & King, R. (1979). Childrearing and children's prosocial initiations toward victims of distress. *Child development,* 50, 319-330.

Democratic Family Practices
In a Nutshell

Families are hierarchical, and thus not everyone has an equal voice, but—if our goal is to foster children for a stronger democratic society—we should aim at being increasingly democratic as our children grow.

• Democratic parenting primarily entails communication with children such that their voices are invited into the family to help make decisions and solve problems; the degree of involvement depends on the developmental appropriateness of the decisions and problems, of course.

• Parents who adopt democratic ways of interacting with their children tend to have their children grow up:
  • with a greater degree of self-esteem
  • more willing to comply with adult requests
  • more willing to engage with others without expecting one-to-one returns
  • with more finely developed consciences
  • with higher degrees of moral reasoning

Young people tend to develop moral reasoning skills when they challenge and dispute one another's moral stances. However, when their discussions are with their parents, their greatest growth takes place when they feel emotionally supported by their parents.

What can we do to foster democratic families?
• Show the same degree of respect to our children that we would want others to show to them.
• Invite children's opinions, to the extent that the topic is something they can handle at their level of development.
• Give children frequent practice in decision-making; limit the complexity of decisions for young children. Enlist their help for family decisions when possible.
• Push children—but push supportively—to think through ideas, concepts, and points of view that they might otherwise not consider.
• Let children know the reasons for our anger or our delight with their actions.

Democratic Parenting
by Marvin W. Berkowitz

When we think about parenting, lots of ideas typically come to mind: love, protection, guidance, discipline, and communication, among others. However, I want to argue that we should be considering the concept of democracy when we think of parenting and families. I hope to offer support for both the power and the relevance of democracy in families, and to suggest some ways we can be effective democratic parents.

When the founders of this great and daring experiment in self-governance that we call a democracy first crafted the blueprints of the United States, they understood that such self-governance depended on the character of its citizens. They also understood that families played a critical role in socializing each subsequent generation to be the kind of citizens necessary for collaborative self-governance. If we want the benefits that democracy can afford us—like liberty, human rights, and equality—then we need citizens who have democratic and moral character. Families, and in particular parents, must play a central role in shaping such future citizens. As George Bernard Shaw once said, "Perhaps the greatest social service that can be rendered by anybody to the country and to mankind is to bring up a family." Those of us who study morality in children understand how critical parenting is in shaping their character. As should be obvious, non-democratic families do not foster democratic character.

In his history of childhood in Western society, Lloyd de Mause (1974) offered a developmental model of historical transitions in parenting which follows the path from adult-focused, hierarchical, power-assertive, and dominant parenting to more child- and rights-focused, egalitarian, and democratic styles. Despite our tendency to venerate, and even worship, the pilgrims who settled what eventually became the United States of America, what we know of their parenting is not for those with weak stomachs. According to de Mause and others, we have come a long way. The final stage de Mause describes is the "helping mode" which he claims began in the mid-20th century. This type of parenting is a servant-leadership orientation that focuses on the child's needs: the parent partners with the child to meet them. In fact, the very concept of children's rights is only a recent historical discovery.

So we can see that a modern enlightened view of parenting is one that recognizes both the moral claim of protecting children's rights and the socio-political claim that we need to raise children of character (both moral and democratic character) for our society to flourish and be the beacon of democracy that it was intended to be. This booklet is about how to parent well

> *"...democratic parents tended to have children who were higher than others in compliance with adults, in development of conscience, and in altruism, self esteem, and moral reasoning maturity"*

and how to raise good children. So let us turn to what we know about one aspect of this parenting recipe…democratic parenting.

A decade ago, John Grych, a child psychologist, and I reviewed the research on parenting and what it revealed about parenting practices that result in moral, pro-social, character development of children (Berkowitz & Grych, 1998). In doing so, we identified what we later called the "fab five." These were five parenting practices that each had a major demonstrated impact on positive child development: nurturance, demandingness, modeling, democratic family process, induction. Those five parenting practices are well-represented in this volume and, we are told, our article was influential on this booklet's composition.

The full name for the democratic practice so influential on children's development of character was "democratic family decision-making and discussion." Research revealed that such democratic parents tended to have children who were higher than others in compliance with adults, in development of conscience, and in altruism, self-esteem, and moral reasoning maturity. In fact, of the five parenting practices, only nurturance (see Diana Baumrind's chapter in this booklet) impacted positive development more broadly. Although it is well accepted that parents should nurture (support, love) their children, it is far more controversial to suggest that parents should be more democratic with their children (see note at end).

Describing Democratic Parenting

There are a few foundational elements to democratic parenting. In character education, we often talk about "head" (understanding, the cognitive component of character), "heart" (caring about, the affective component) and "hand" (acting upon, the behavioral component). We can identify a parallel "head, heart and hand" of educators: understanding what character is, caring about instilling character in students, and teaching the skills to make it happen. Likewise, we can identify the "head, heart and hand" of parenting for character in general, and of democratic parenting in particular.

The parent's "head" of democratic parenting has to do with understanding (1) that children are autonomous human beings with their own rights, (2) that power can be distributed in different ways in a family, and (3) that democratic parenting is good for children and for society. The "heart" of democratic parenting is valuing democracy in general and the democratic process. It also has to do with caring about being the best parent one can and caring deeply about what is right and good for children; it is willingness and commitment to being a shepherd—a guide for the lifelong path that the child's development will follow. Some people and some societies see children as a burden, others as a potential resource (e.g., workforce). We are arguing for commitment to children as a moral responsibility for their welfare and development, much as de Mause did in identifying the helping mode of parenting. My colleague Bill Puka once posited the notion of "developmental love." By this he meant that one way to show love for a child is to dedicate oneself to his or her healthiest development. The "heart" also entails faith; that is, a belief that a long-term commitment to democratic parenting will indeed lead to the kind of child development that one intends to produce. The "hand" of democratic parenting is the set of parenting skills necessary to be democratic in one's daily parenting behaviors. These include certain communication skills, the ability to make children feel safe and supported especially during disagreements, etc. I will turn to these in more detail in a moment. First, however, let us take a closer look at what democratic parenting really looks like.

The core of democratic parenting is an orientation toward certain forms of communication, especially in problem-solving and decision-making situations. Democratic parents both (1) value their children's

autonomy and respect their rights and
perspectives and (2) understand that in
doing so they are optimally fostering their
children's moral and civic development.
Therefore they "respect children's voices
as meaningful contributions to family
discussions, decisions, and conflict resolution
processes" (Berkowitz & Grych, 1998, p. 385-
6). They also understand that through their
demonstrations of respect they are fostering
the development of those character traits listed
above as outcomes of democratic parenting

> *"... in doing so they are optimally fostering their children's moral and civic development"*

(e.g., altruism, conscience, and moral reasoning maturity). In other
words, they realize that democratic parenting is not only just, it is also
developmentally effective. Because they realize this, democratic parents
"let children know that their voices are valued and provide affective
support for their participation in family discussions" (ibid, p. 386).

That latter point about affective support is worth belaboring. My
earliest research was on the promotion of moral reasoning maturity
through peer discussions. The most developmentally productive
discussions were often quite contentious, with children and adolescents
cognitively grappling and attempting to "win" the "debate." This seemed
to really stretch children's thinking about right and wrong and produced
significant development.

However, when we tried to apply this model to parent-child
moral discussions the picture changed. The key difference was that
children did not develop when their moral discussions with parents
were contentious. Rather children needed to be couched in a context of
feeling emotionally supported by their parent(s). The discourse looked
different, more like respectful disagreement in which both parties
knew there was no risk to the relationship. This seems critical to how
democratic families disagree, especially about potentially emotionally
charged issues. Larry Nucci has much to contribute to this issue in his
chapter in this booklet.

Another of this booklet's authors, Diana Baumrind (1991), shed
important light on this many years ago. Baumrind has spent decades
studying the dimensions and effects of different styles of parenting.
One style she identified was labeled "democratic." She defined this as

being high on *supportive control* ("considerateness, responsive discipline, principled use of rational explanations to influence adolescent intellectual stimulation, and encouragement of individuation" p. 751), with a moderate use of more assertive control but low on more directive/conventional control strategies. As Baumrind describes such parents, they are "more responsive than demanding, are agentic but not officious, and set limits when necessary, although their preference is to be lenient" (p. 752). Others who have studied such parents have found them to be warm and supportive, low in anxiety, and low in power assertion, with rules being created jointly by parents and children. In other words, democratic parents love their children, feel comfortable with them and in their roles as parents, and do not seem to need to

> *"democratic parents... do not seem to need to exert their authority in a hierarchical manner"*

exert their authority in a hierarchical manner. Such parents tend to have very healthy children, although in adolescence they may experiment more with drugs.

Democratic parenting is thus justified in three ways: as a form of just respect for children; as a means of socializing responsible democratic citizens; and as an effective way to educate moral children. We have also established that democratic parents need to understand democracy and democratic parenting and its justifications and they need to care deeply about children and democratic society. It is now time to look more closely at the "hand" or skills of democratic parenting. How does one become a democratic parent?

What You Can Do
• Respect and Love Children

Democratic parenting and democracy in general both depend upon respect for others (in this case respect for children). When we think of respect, we often think of the Golden Rule. In their book on *Emotionally Intelligent Parenting*, Maurice Elias and his colleagues (1999) transform the Golden Rule into the 24-Karat Golden Rule: that is "Do unto your children as you would have other people do unto your children" (p. 1). As they point out, we often allow ourselves to act on a lower standard toward our children than we expect of others (neighbors, teachers, etc.). So one good way to test your level of respect for your child is to ask yourself how you would feel and react if someone else were behaving toward him or her the way you are.

> *"...the second fundamental tenet of democratic parenting is that parents need to actively invite children's input..."*

We have also seen from the research that respect is not enough. Children need to be and feel loved and supported, in addition to being respected. As parents we need to create a constant substrate of affection, not make it contingent upon their specific behaviors and misbehaviors, and we must communicate our affection clearly to our children. We can't forget to clearly express our love to them.

• Welcome and Solicit Children's Voices

There is an old saying that children should be seen and not heard. That may be the exact opposite of democratic parenting, at least on the "heard" part. For a family to be democratic, two fundamental and related things need to happen. First, children need to believe that their voices are valued and welcomed—that their parents want to know what they think and will seriously consider their input. Oftentimes, however, as much as we may genuinely want to include children in family decisions, discussions, and problem-solving, we may forget to ask them or may be too hurried or stressed to be willing to expend the time it takes to have such conversations. So, the second fundamental tenet of democratic parenting is that parents need to actively invite children's input; they need to ask children to speak up and be heard. Of course, as in any social group, this openness to input must be authentic. Children will quickly figure out if you are just humoring them or paying lip service to valuing their voices. We will introduce some structured ways of inviting children's voices in a moment.

• Be Developmentally Appropriate

Children at different developmental levels require different degrees of structure in invitations to chime in. Furthermore, what may be appropriate for an adolescent to discuss may not be appropriate for a younger child, or it may not be appropriate for any child. It may be appropriate to ask a child what the family should have for dinner, but not whether parents should itemize their tax returns or take out a second mortgage. And giving a young child an open-ended option ("what do you want for dinner?") may not be prudent. Rather, limit the options to make it easier for them to decide ("do you want hamburgers or spaghetti for dinner?"). Walking into Baskin-Robbins and asking a pre-schooler what flavor he or she wants could lead to hours of vacillation. A better strategy would be to ask young children which of two or three flavors they want, knowing which two or three flavors they like most. As they get older, the choices we give them can be more complex and open-ended.

> *"As they get older, the choices we give them can be more complex and open-ended"*

• Be Socrates

We are not advocating that children get veto power, nor that you should only have one child so that children can never be in the majority in the family democracy. Nor are we advocating installing a democratic government in your household. Rather we are advocating adopting some principles of democracy in your parenting. One of them is to be Socratic. As Bill Puka suggests with his notion of developmental love, we need to be guides and gurus for our children's development. We can do that within democratic structures by being Socratic; that is, by using discussion to get them to consider critical concepts and facts that might otherwise be missed.

A variety of strands in psychology emphasize the power of reflecting on reasons for choices and decisions. Children need to learn what a justification is, and what counts as a good reason; they also need to learn to use reasoning to justify their demands, claims, and assertions. Parents need to ask children "why" they think it is a good idea to open presents on Christmas eve rather than Christmas day, to get a pet dog, or to be the one to get the last piece of pizza. Then discuss the reasons and see if you can come to agreement on the soundness and validity of their justifications.

The parenting practice of induction (one of the Fab Five mentioned earlier; see Marilyn Watson's contribution in this booklet) is also relevant here. Induction means that, when parents are either praising or reprimanding their children, they focus on giving a reason for their praise or displeasure by highlighting the consequences of the child's actions for another's emotions (e.g., "I am so proud of you because you told Aunt Martha that you liked the birthday present and that really made her happy" or "I am so angry with you because you hit Linda and now she is sad and crying"). In other words, in family discussions and negotiations, be sure to direct children's attention toward reasons for behaviors, the consequences of actions (especially their own actions), and other people's feelings.

• Don't Be Napoleon

Democratic character comes not from learning about democracy as much as it does from experiencing democracy; that is, from experiencing the power of your voice in collaborative decision-making. Families tend to be hierarchical, often for good reasons. Parents wield power and children are subject to it. This is not a good source of the formation of future democratic citizens. Just as in schools, adults in families tend to make all the decisions and solve all the problems themselves. We waste so many opportunities to enlist our children in these decisions and deliberations. Parents need to look for opportunities to welcome children into family discussions and deliberations. Just as parents find opportunities to name objects ("See the doggie") and colors ("That ball is red") to

> *"Each time we act unilaterally we steal a developmental opportunity from the child."*

help children develop language, they need to find opportunities to invite children to contribute to decisions ("Which sweater do you think Grandpa would like best?") and solutions ("What do you think would be a good way to make Alex feel better?"), rather than just doing it oneself. Each time we act unilaterally we steal a developmental opportunity from the child. Of course, all this has to be within reason, or life will grind to a halt as we negotiate every choice and solution. Pick your spots!

• Create or Adopt a Family Problem-Solving Method

Having a clear method for decision-making and/or problem-solving can be very helpful. In his book *Raising Good Children*, Thomas Lickona recommends what he calls a "fairness approach." There are ten steps to this method for achieving mutual understanding of the nature of and perspectives on the problem, then solving the problem, and finally following through to monitor the success and implementation of the solution. In all steps, parents and children are equally involved in collaboratively moving through the process. Some parents like to write and sign a contract or agreement that describes the result of the problem-solving process, and it often ends up on the refrigerator door as a reminder and resource.

• Be Values Driven

While democracy is an excellent social system, it is not flawless. Winston Churchill once opined that democracy is the worst form of government humans have ever created…except for all the others. Democracy does allow for injustices to be done (and justified) by the majority to the minority. So it is important to have a values base for your family in general and for your democratic

> *"It is important to know what your most central moral values are."*

processes in particular. Many years ago, I had the privilege of working on Lawrence Kohlberg's Just Community Schools project. This project was an experiment in high school democracy. We created small alternative schools within larger high schools and endowed them with the freedom of self-governance. One person, one vote; teacher, student, administrator. But these mini-democracies had two guiding values: justice and community. All community decisions were supposed to try to maximize justice and to build a sense of community.

It is important in your family to know what you hold most dear. It is important to know what your most central moral values are. They may be derived directly from your faith tradition, or may be adopted or adapted from a variety of sources. Wherever they originate, they should be invoked as the litmus test for your important family decisions. As parents you should raise them and ask questions such as "is that fair to everyone?", "does that show respect for our neighbors?", or "how is that a loving thing to do to her?"

• Check-In

Do not assume success. It is a good idea to check in periodically both on the success of prior decisions and solutions and on the degree to which children and parents feel in general that the family is operating fairly. But be forewarned that the very notion of fairness (justice) is a developmental concept. What is fair to a pre-schooler (idiosyncratic and/or selfish) is not fair to an elementary school child (stubborn radical equality) and is different from what is fair to an adolescent (balancing of legitimate claims and perspectives). Even if you and your child are on different wavelengths, and even if you can't come to an agreement, you are still engaging in open, respectful, and egalitarian discourse.

> *"... what is fair to a pre-schooler is not fair to an elementary school child and is different from what is fair to an adolescent"*

Conclusion

Democratic parenting is justified for three main reasons: (1) because it is just and respectful of children; (2) because it is a context for the development of civic character and future responsible democratic citizens; and (3) because research has shown that it produces a wide range of desirable moral and social characteristics in children. Such parenting requires an understanding of democracy, children's rights, and democratic parenting strategies, and it requires an authentic concern for children's development and fairness, and a command of the parenting skills necessary to be an effective democratic parent. Those skills include induction, collaborative decision-making, and the ability to adapt to the development level of the child.

Note

Interestingly, John Grych and I later wrote a parallel paper for teachers, when Tom Lickona (see his chapter in this volume) suggested that the Fab Five parenting behaviors applied equally well to education. Teachers can also engage in all of the same behaviors, and evidence is beginning to show that they are just as relevant to schools as they are to families. When both families and schools engage in parallel, research-supported practices of raising and teaching children we are more likely to successfully raise the next generation of responsible democratic citizens and adults.

References

Baumrind, D. (1991). Parenting styles and adolescent development. In R.M. Lerner, A.C. Petersen, & J. Brooks-Gunn (Eds.), *Encyclopedia of adolescence: Volume 2* (pp. 746-758). New York: Garland.

Berkowitz, M.W. & Grych, J.H. (1998). Fostering goodness: teaching parents to facilitate children's moral development. *Journal of moral education*, 27, 371-391.

DeMause, L. (1974). *The evolution of childhood*. In L. de Mause (Ed.), The history of childhood (pp. 1-74). New York: Harper and Row.

Elias, M.J., Tobias, S.E., & Friedlander, B.S. (1999). *Emotionally intelligent parenting: How to raise a self-disciplined, responsible, socially skilled child*. NY: Three Rivers Press.

Lickona, T. (1983). *Raising good children*. NY: Bantam Books.

The Domains of Social Reasoning
In a Nutshell

Understanding that there are three or four "ways" of reasoning in regard to social and moral issues can help parents both raise children of character and lessen the intensity of parent-child (especially adolescent) disputes.

One of these ways of reasoning is called the *moral domain*, which has to do with matters of justice, fairness, and human welfare. As early as age four or five, children understand that moral transgressions—like taking something that belongs to someone else—are wrong. Even if adults tried to convince a child that such a transgression was acceptable, children would be reluctant to accept their approval of such actions. We do not easily change children's minds about moral issues.

Children's reasoning about issues in the *conventional domain* is very different from the way they reason about morality. Conventional issues are not necessarily right or wrong in themselves, even though many of them are of tremendous importance in society. Approval by authority figures is what makes conventional issues right or wrong. Conventional matters entail actions that facilitate our social interactions, such as our "manners" (the way we dress, speak, and so forth). There was a time not long ago that a man with an earring—an issue of convention rather than of morality—was looked upon with disdain. Today, if the earring is small, that man does not bring attention to himself in most social circles. However, a man who goes to a playground and pushes children off the swings is disdained today as he would have been thirty years ago or two centuries ago, because of the moral domain issue of unfairness and the possibility of physical harm.

In this chapter, researcher and educator Larry Nucci outlines the moral and conventional domains, and introduces two others—the personal domain, regarding issues over which we, and we alone, should decide, and the prudential domain, regarding issues of personal safety. Professor Nucci also discusses how we as parents can both be more effective and avoid conflict if we are aware of the different domains and what they mean in the context of parent/child relationships. (Note that a certain amount of conflict in families is important, in part because of the opportunities it affords us to teach our children.)

Parental disciplinary responses should reflect the domain of the behavior. For example, reminding children about rules is only effective in conventional issues ("Remember that even though Joe is our neighbor, when you are at school you need to call him Mr. Spooner, because he is a teacher").

Explaining an action's effect on others is of great importance in moral issues ("You really hurt Patti's feelings when you took her dog Bailey from her"), but it has little effect in issues of convention.

Young children learn from their disputes with other children. Parents can best help their growth *not* by stepping in and solving or stopping disputes, but rather by helping them work toward fair solutions to their problems.

As children grow older, most areas of conflict with parents do not entail the moral domain, because of our basic agreement on such issues. Most parent-adolescent disputes entail those areas that the child considers personal (whether I get a tatoo, or wear my hair a certain way, or have clothing lying around my room to the extent that it is hard to see the floor) but the parent considers an issue of convention ("People like us just don't do that!").

Especially when disputes straddle the personal and the conventional domains, the most effective way to foster character development takes place when adults begin to negotiate with their children and, especially when the children are adolescents, gradually but increasingly give children freedom to make choices. On the whole, young people who have been given significant freedom to make decisions in the personal domain are more open with their parents about their personal lives.

The Domains of Social Reasoning
How We Think about Right and Wrong and Why It Matters to Parents
by Larry Nucci

The goal of every parent is to raise what my colleague Tom Lickona refers to as "good children." Over the past 30 years we have learned that one of the major factors contributing to developing good children is attention to the domains of social reasoning (Hasebe, Nucci & Nucci, 2004; Smetana, 2005). These domains provide frameworks for making sense out of the social world (Turiel, 2006). We have discovered that the willingness of children and adolescents to accept and benefit from parental authority entails matching parenting behaviors with the domain of the child's behaviors and decisions (Nucci, Hasebe & Dyer, 2005; Smetana, Crean & Campione-Barr, 2005). Let us look at the basic domains of social development, and then at how understanding these domains might help parents both diminish conflict with their children and help them along the path to being "good."

The Domains:
Moral, Conventional, Personal (Prudential)

Morality and Convention

Central to raising a good child is fostering a sense of right and wrong. The way we think about morality is distinct from the way we think about social convention; they belong to different domains (Turiel, 2006). Morality is about fairness, and how we treat others. The child's morality emerges from his or her experiences with actions that have effects upon other people. For example, when we hit others

> *"Morality is about fairness, and how we treat others"*

with force, we hurt them. Very young children are capable of observing the effects of acts such as unprovoked hitting, as well as their own experiences as victims, and coming to the conclusion that an act such as hitting is wrong. What makes hitting wrong is not the existence of a social rule, but the hurtful effects of the act. A child or adolescent's reasoning about morality is determined by her concepts about fairness and human welfare. With development, children apply their moral knowledge to broader and more abstract issues of justice and human rights.

In contrast with morality, there is nothing intrinsically right or wrong with actions defined by social conventions. For example there is nothing inherently better about a student calling a teacher by his last name and title, Mr. Nucci, instead of his first name, Larry. In order for a student to know that it is wrong to refer to Mr. Nucci as Larry, there would have to be a social rule about addressing teachers, and the student would have to be aware of the social rule. Rules of this kind are social conventions. Conventions are arbitrary in that the wrong or right of a convention can vary. For example, there are schools where it is perfectly acceptable to address the teacher by his first name. Conventions exist through the social agreement of people who are part of a social system. Conventions serve to provide organization and predictability to our interactions in social settings. For example, without conventions, it would be hard to organize a family dinner. A child or adolescent's reasoning about social convention is determined by his underlying understanding of the connection between convention and social organization.

> *"Conventions serve to provide organization and predictability to our interactions in social settings"*

Interviews with children show that they reason differently about morality and convention beginning as early as two and a half years of age (Smetana & Braeges, 1987). The distinction children make between morality and convention is nicely illustrated in the following example. The excerpt is from an interview conducted in the U.S. Virgin Islands (Nucci, Turiel & Encarnacion-Gawrych, 1983), with a 4-year-old girl talking about her perceptions of spontaneously occurring events at her preschool.

Moral Issue
Did you see what happened?
Yes. They were playing and John hit him too hard.
Is that something you are supposed to do or not supposed to do?
Not so hard to hurt.

Is there a rule about that?
Yes.
What is the rule?
You're not to hit hard.
What if there were no rule about hitting hard, would it be all right to do then?
No.
Why not?
Because he could get hurt and start to cry.

Conventional Issue
Did you see what just happened?
Yes. They were noisy.
Is that something you are supposed to or not supposed to do?
Not do.
Is there a rule about that?
Yes. We have to be quiet.
What if there were no rule, would it be all right to do then?
Yes.
Why?
Because there is no rule.

Research conducted in a variety of countries (including Brazil, Mexico, Zambia, Indonesia, Japan, Korea, and The People's Republic of China) has demonstrated that the distinction between morality and convention is cross-cultural (Turiel, 2006). Moreover, studies conducted with devout Jewish and Christian children and adolescents have demonstrated that children make similar kinds of distinctions with respect to religious rules (Nucci, 2001). Children in these studies stated that it would be all right for members of their faith to engage in actions contrary to what is currently regulated by religious conventions—such as the day of worship, wearing head coverings, women leading religious services—if there were no longer a religious rule about the act. On the other hand, actions that are moral transgressions—such as unprovoked hitting, stealing, or damaging another person's reputation—were judged to be wrong even if there were no religious rule or scriptural injunction prohibiting the act. In sum, the way human beings think about concepts like fairness or harm to others—what we know as the moral domain—is very different from the way we think about conventional domain issues, like table manners or the way we address people.

The Personal Domain

Morality and convention are in turn distinct from behaviors and choices that are matters of privacy and personal preference. Reasoning about such issues falls within what is referred to as the personal domain (Nucci, 1996). The personal domain refers to actions that form the private aspects of one's life, such as the contents of a diary, and issues that are matters of preference and choice (e.g., friends, music, hairstyle) rather than right or wrong. Control over the personal domain emerges from the need to establish boundaries between the self and others, and is critical to the formation of children's personal autonomy and individual identity (Nucci, 1996). Interview studies conducted in a range of cultural settings including northeastern Brazil, Colombia, Hong Kong, China, and Japan as well as the United States have shown that children and adolescents judge personal issues to be up to them, and them alone (Nucci, 2001). Research has also shown that most parents across cultures allow a certain amount of privacy and personal choice, even to children as young as three to four-years-of-age (Smetana, 2005). The reasons that children and their parents provide for why behaviors and decisions should be treated as personal and within the child's jurisdiction focus on the role of such choices in developing the child's autonomy and personal identity, and the child or adolescent's moral right to have such discretion (Smetana, 2005).

> *"The personal domain refers to actions that form the private aspects of one's life"*

The Prudential Domain

> *"the prudential domain relates to actions that have consequences for the health and well-being on the individual"*

What we refer to as the prudential domain relates to actions that have consequences for the health and well-being of the individual. The capacity to make prudential judgments is a function of cognitive development, social knowledge, and psychological integrity. Young children are clearly incapable of making wise judgments about a range of issues—from education to media exposure— that affect their well-being. In research conducted on children's rights, scholars distinguish between nurturance rights and independence rights (Ruck, Abramovitch, & Keating, 1998). Independence rights are analogous to what we refer to as the personal domain. Nurturance rights include the set of protective actions children are entitled to receive from parents including provision of food, clothing, shelter, and love as well as protection and guidance from potential sources of harm such as corrosive media, youth gangs, addictive substances, and poor academic choices. Studies conducted in countries as diverse as Brazil, China, Japan, Korea, United States, and Canada indicate that children and parents both expect, and accept, parental authority over actions that fall within this prudential category (Smetana, 2005). However, this expectation of parental control shifts dramatically with age, such that within the United States, the majority of adolescents argue for personal control over these prudential decisions by roughly age 15 or 16 (Smetana, 2005).

Implications for Parenting
One Size Does *Not* Fit All

The most important implication of these domains of social reasoning is that parents cannot take a single-minded approach to their children's social behavior. Parental statements about rules and social expectations are appropriate. When such statements are made about social conventions, they help give structure to a child's social development. Statements such as, "Remember to chew with your mouth closed," "We don't wear jeans to Church because the Church is not a playground," or "We eat dinner at the same time because I can't be cooking separate meals for everyone, and besides it is the only time during the day when we get together as a family" inform the child of social expectations and the social organizational function that conventions serve.

Children's morality, however, is not based on knowledge about rules. Nor is it based on the demands of authority. Despite the fact that such explanations help children understand conventions, telling children about the rules (e.g., It's a sin to lie) has essentially no impact with regard to moral growth. Trying to directly instruct children about morality by telling them how they should act might buy momentary compliance, but it will have little long-term payoff. Instead, a child's moral development is affected by experiences (including conversations) having to do with feelings, and thoughts about the ways that actions affect people. Parental statements focusing on actions and perspective taking such as: "That really hurt Mike," "How would you feel

> *Parental statements focusing on actions and perspective taking... are appropriate adult responses to moral transgressions*

if someone had called you a name like that?" "Do you think it is fair that you have twice as much as she does?" are viewed by children as effective and appropriate adult responses to moral transgressions.

Parents can contribute to moral development with young children by serving as mediators in disputes, helping them to listen to one another and to figure out a fair solution. Stepping in and solving disputes, however, does not contribute to development, and is not generally appreciated by children (Killen, 1991). Finally, parents contribute to children's moral development by providing an emotional environment that fosters compassion and empathy. Young children in particular flourish in environments that are emotionally supportive and that foster a sense of trust. Marilyn Watson, Marvin Berkowitz, and Diana Baumrind all discuss this in their contributions to this booklet. Households that have high negative emotions, especially anger, increase the likelihood that children will construct a view of the world as malevolent and unpredictable. The moral perspectives of children and adolescents who hold such a worldview are often egocentric and exploitive. In a similar vein, responding to moral transgressions with harsh punishments has little effect on moral development, and may simply redirect the child's anger at the parent rather than toward thinking about the harm that was caused by the behavior.

Knowing When to Say "Yes"

Parental authority is not the same thing as parental power. Parental power comes from physical size, control over resources, and societal support. Parental authority comes from the child. Establishing and maintaining parental authority is a process of maintaining legitimacy.

Children and adolescents across a broad spectrum of cultures from North and South America to Asia maintain that parents have jurisdiction over children's moral, conventional, and prudential behaviors (Smetana, 2005). Across this same range of cultures, however, children do not see it as legitimate for parents to exert control over the child's personal domain (Nucci, 2001). Indeed, adolescent perceptions of parental intrusion into decision-making and control over the child's personal issues (e.g., reading the child's diary, controlling their friendships and music choices) are associated with psychological symptoms of anxiety, depression, and eating disorders in the US and Japan (Hasebe, Nucci and Nucci, 2004), and among middle class African-Americans (Smetana, Campione-Barr &Daddis, 2004).

> *"Clearly, the personal domain is an area where parents should tread lightly"*

Clearly, the personal domain is an area where parents should tread lightly. Complicating the matter, however, are the developmental dynamics at work from late childhood into middle adolescence during which time children are expanding the range of behaviors they consider to be personal matters rather than issues of family convention or prudence (Smetana, 2005). Cross-cultural studies have also shown that parents have similar notions and expect to turn over more and more decision-making regarding such things as bedtimes, personal hygiene, and dating to their children as they get older. However, parents tend to be about six months behind the pace of demands by their children. Disputes over issues that sit on the cusp of convention, prudence and the personal (what Judith Smetana refers to as "ambiguously personal") comprise virtually all of the content of adolescent-parent disputes (Smetana, 2005). Adolescents and parents report almost no disputes over issues of morality, basic societal conventions, or clear prudential issues such as alcohol or drug abuse, all of which are viewed as within the legitimate sphere of parental authority.

How parents handle the conflicts that straddle the different domains has been the subject of recent research. The healthiest pattern is where parents negotiate with their adolescent children, and work toward gradually giving more control over such behaviors and choices to the adolescent. The least healthy is a parental pattern that fits what Diana Baumrind refers to as 'authoritarian" parenting (see her contribution in this booklet) in which no distinction is made by the parent among the personal and other behavioral categories such that the parent attempts to control the full range of behaviors leaving little room for the adolescent to flourish (Smetana, 1995).

Maintaining Communication: A 2-way street

One of the primary predictors of adolescent engagement in risk-taking and delinquent behavior is the degree to which parents know about the activities of their children (Fletcher, Steinberg, Williams-Wheeler, 2004). The greater the degree of parental knowledge the lower the amount of risk-taking and negative behaviors engaged in by adolescents. It turns out, however, that parental knowledge is less a result of parental monitoring than it is of adolescent disclosure (Stattin & Kerr, 2000). In other words, if parents really want to know what their children are doing, their chances of success are greater if they establish an appropriate level of freedom in the personal domain than if they try to monitor and control their children's activities. One of the factors impacting adolescents' willingness to disclose is their perceptions of their parents' efforts to control the adolescents' personal domain (Smetana, Metzger, Gettman, & Campione-Barr, 2006). Adolescents who perceive their parents as less intrusive are more willing in general to disclose personal information to their parents, even when it concerns involvement in drinking or sexual behavior. Adolescents who can be open to their parents are less likely to be engaged in negative behaviors.

> *Adolescents who perceive their parents as less intrusive are less likely to be engaged in negative behaviors*

The links between parental control, adolescent depression and disclosure were recently revealed in a longitudinal study by Stattin and Kerr (2006) in which they found that depressed adolescents invoked higher efforts by parents to monitor and control the personal domains of their children, which led to greater efforts toward secrecy by the children and consequently higher levels of depression and negative behaviors, which invoked even greater degrees of parental monitoring and control. This negative spiral continued over time for as long as the study was able to follow.

Concluding Thoughts

In this brief article, I have introduced social cognitive domains of reasoning and described their connection to positive parenting. What we have learned from the study of children's development is that our concepts of morality, societal norms and personal values are constructed within different conceptual frameworks: that is, the actual way we think about societal norms, or personal values, is different from the way we think through issues of morality. These different ways of thinking stem from and account for different aspects of our social worlds. The implication for optimal parenting is that our approach to our children should take these domains into account. Part of the art of raising a good child is to know when to set limits, and when to give over decision-making and authority to your child. This balancing act contributes toward the child's development as an autonomous individual. It also increases the chances of the child becoming someone who treats others fairly and compassionately, respects social rules, and makes wise decisions when it comes to personal safety and well-being. These issues arise daily as parents weigh their role in response to questions about bedtimes, sleepovers, household chores, manners, homework, and weightier concerns such as sexuality, alcohol and drug use, shoplifting and delinquency.

References

Fletcher AC, Steinberg L, Williams-Wheeler, M. (2004). Parental influences on adolescent problem behavior: Revisiting Stattin and Kerr, *Child Development*, 75, 781-796.

Hasebe, Y., Nucci, L. & Nucci, M. (2004). Parental control of the personal domain and adolescent symptoms of psychopathology: A cross-national study in the U.S. and Japan. *Child Development*, 75, 1-14.

Killen, M. (1991). Social and moral development in early childhood. In W. Kurtines & J. Gewirtz (Eds.), *Handbook of moral behavior and development: Vol. 2, Research* (pp. 115-138). Hillsdale, NJ: Erlbaum.

Nucci, L. (1996). Morality and the personal sphere of actions. In E. Reed, E. Turiel, & T. Brown (Eds.), *Values and knowledge* (pp. 41-60). Hillsdale, NJ.: Lawrence Erlbaum.

Nucci, L. (2001). *Education in the moral domain.* Cambridge, UK: Cambridge University Press.

Nucci, L., Hasebe, Y., & Lins-Dyer, T. (2005). Adolescent psychological well-being and parental control of the personal. In J. Smetana (Ed.). *Changing boundaries of parental authority in adolescence* (pp. 17-30). San Francisco: Jossey-Bass.

Nucci, L., Turiel, E., & Encarnacion-Gawrych, G. (1983). Children's social interactions and social concepts in the Virgin Islands. *Journal of Cross-Cultural Psychology,* 14, 469-487.

Ruck, M., Abramovitch, R., & Keating, D. (1998). Children's and adolescents' understanding of rights: Balancing nurturance and self-determination. *Child Development,* 64, 404-417.

Smetana, J. G. (1995). Parenting styles and conceptions of parental authority during adolescence, *Child Development,* 66, 299-316.

Smetana, J. G. (2005). Adolescent-parent conflict: Resistance and subversion as developmental process. In L. Nucci (Ed.), *Conflict, contradiction and contrarian elements in moral development and education.* (pp.69 – 91). Mahwah, NJ: Lawrence Erlbaum.

Smetana, J. G., Braeges, J. L., The development of toddlers' moral and conventional judgments, *Merril-Palmer Quarterly-Journal of Developmental Psychology,* 36, 329-346.

Smetana, J. G., Campione-Barr, N., & Daddis, C. (2004). Developmental and longitudinal antecedents of family decision-making: Defining health behavioral autonomy for African American adolescents. *Child Development,* 75, 1418-1434.

Smetana, J. G., Crean, H., & Campione-Barr, N. (2005). Adolescents' and parents' changing conceptions of parental authority. In J. Smetana (Ed.). *Changing boundaries of parental authority in adolescence* (pp. 31-46). San Francisco: Jossey-Bass.

Smetana, J. G., Metzger, A., Gettman, D. C., & Campione-Barr, N. (2006). Disclosure and secrecy in adolescent-parent relationships. *Child Development,* 77, 201-217.

Stattin H, Kerr M. (2000). Parental monitoring: A reinterpretation. *International Journal of Psychology* 35 153-153.

Stattin, H., & Kerr (May, 2006). Disclosure in the context of parents' attempts to get knowledge. A person-centered approach. Paper presented at the annual meeting of the European Association for Research on Adolescence, Antalya, Turkey.

About the Authors

Diana Baumrind

Diana Baumrind is a research psychologist and the principal investigator for the Family Socialization and Developmental Competence Project in the Institute of Human Development at the University of California, Berkeley. Her primary professional interests are in the areas of family socialization and developmental competence, health and adolescent substance use, and ethics. Professor Baumrind has authored scores of professional articles and given numerous invited lectures; she has been honored formally by both the American Psychological Association and the National Institute of Health. She has been writing about "parental control and parental love" since 1965.

Marvin W. Berkowitz

Marvin W. Berkowitz is a developmental psychologist whose primary interest is in promoting children's development toward becoming healthy, happy adults who are also effective moral agents and contributors to their societies. Berkowitz is the Sanford N. McDonnell Professor of Character Education at the University of Missouri-St. Louis, where he directs the McDonnell Leadership Academy in Character Education for school principals. His research interests are in the areas of character education, moral development, and prevention of risky behaviors. He is a member of CSEE's Advisory Board for Moral Education and a trainer for CSEE's Moral Development Team.

Tom Lickona

Tom Lickona is a developmental psychologist and professor of education at the State University of New York at Cortland, where he directs the Center for the 4th and 5th Rs (Respect and Responsibility). He has authored nine books on character development, including *Raising Good Children*, *Educating for Character*, and *Character Matters*. His books on character development include *Raising Good Children*, *Character Matters*, and, with Matthew Davidson, *Smart & Good High Schools* (www.cortland.edu/character). He is a member of CSEE's Advisory Board for Moral Education and a trainer for CSEE's Moral Development Team.

Larry Nucci

Larry Nucci is Professor Emeritus of Educational Psychology at the University of Illinois at Chicago. He currently teaches in the Graduate School of Education at the University of California, Berkeley. He is Editor of the journal *Human Development* and on the editorial boards of the *Journal for Research in Character Education* and *Cognitive Development*. Nucci is a member of the Educational Advisory Committee of the Character Education Partnership and a member of the Board of Advisors on Moral Education for the Council for Spiritual and Ethical Education. He is the author of *Education in the Moral Domain* (2001), and editor of *The Handbook of Moral and Character Education* (in press); *Conflict, Contradiction and Contrarian Elements in Moral Development and Education* (2005); *Culture, Thought* and *Development* (2000); and *Moral Development and Character Education: A Dialogue* (1989).

Marilyn Watson

Marilyn Watson recently retired from the Developmental Studies Center, where she headed the center's National Teacher Education Project and was the program director for the Child Development Project (CDP). The Child Development Project has been called one of the most successful moral development programs ever implemented. Watson has spent the past two decades working with educators to promote children's social, intellectual, and moral development. She is the author (with classroom teacher Laura Ecken) of *Learning to Trust* (2003) and of CSEE's 2007 publication, *Discipline for Moral Growth*. Watson is a member of CSEE's Advisory Board for Moral Education and a trainer for CSEE's Moral Development Team.

Acknowledgments

The following parents graciously gave their time to read chapters of this work and provide helpful comments. Some of these are also members of CSEE's Moral Development Team:

Bett Alter, Washington, Connecticut
Susan Bauska, Tacoma, Washington
Lynn Hanke, New York, New York
Kimberly Hockstein, Smyrna, Georgia
Doris Marks, Beaverton, Oregon
Mike Pardee, Houston, Texas
Carolyn Ragland, Baltimore, MD
Jonathan Rosenshine, New York, New York
Julie Sherman, Brentwood, Tenessee
Julie Stevens, Portland, Oregon

We are also indebted to the following for their assistance in putting this work together:

Jennifer Aanderud, Portland, Oregon
Michael Cerkovnik, Ballwin, Missouri
Scott Gartlan, Concord, North Carolina
Adriana Murphy. Rockville, Maryland

About CSEE

The Council for Spiritual and Ethical Education is a century-old association of independent schools in the United States and Canada that assists schools in their efforts for character education, spiritual growth, and the development of ethical leaders for tomorrow's world.

CSEE provides resources and educational opportunities to elementary, middle, and secondary schools in the areas of its mission.

CSEE resources include national and regional workshops and conferences, consultation, and a variety of publications. Details are available at http://www.csee.org

CSEE is a non-profit 501 (c) 3 educational association that is supported by school membership fees and the generosity of those who believe in our work. To help support the moral and spiritual development of young people through research-based best practices in a non-sectarian framework, visit http://www.csee.org

This booklet for parents was conceived and written to help schools and parents work together on one of the most important responsbilities they have.